W9-COH-865

FOUR CAME HOME

The Gripping Story of the Survivors of Jimmy Doolittle's Two Lost Crews

CARROLL V. GLINES

PICTORIAL HISTORIES PUBLISHING COMPANY, INC.
Missoula, Montana

First Published in paperback in 1981

PRINTED IN THE UNITED STATES OF AMERICA

First Printing Revised Edition: December 1995

TYPOGRAPHY & DESIGN: Arrow Graphics, Missoula, Montana
COVER ART: James Farmer, Glendora, California

Pictorial Histories Publishing Company, Inc.
713 South Third Street West
Missoula, Montana 59801

Downed Doolittle's Raiders pose with their Japanese captors in China. From left are Cpl. Jacob DeShazer, Sgt. Harold A. Spatz, Lt. Robert L. Hite, Lt. William G. Farrow, and Lt. George Barr. AIR FORCE MUSEUM

JAPANESE KILL U. S. FLYERS
CAPTURED IN RAID ON TOKIO

AGREE TO NEW HOUSE VOTE ON PAY-AS-GO TAX

Draft Rival Plans in Committee.

BY WILLIAM STRAND

[Chicago Tribune Press Service.]

Washington, D. C., April 21. — The ...

Easter 'Gift' of Greetings Starts Today

TWO PAGES OF NAMES.

...

ACROSS THE NATION'S HEART

THE SHEDDING OF INNOCENT BLOOD

SWORN

Japanese Beasts

(An Editorial)

The White House announces that the American flyers who bombed Japan a year ago and were taken prisoner by the Japanese have been sentenced to death and some of them have been executed.

Their blood cries for vengeance. If anything had been needed after Pearl Harbor to steel the American people to a determination to destroy Japanese power for all time, this hideous crime has filled the gap.

...

F. D. R. BRANDS ENEMY ACTION AS 'BARBAROUS'

Nippon Won't Tell How Many Died.

[Pictures on page 8.]

Washington, D. C., April 21 (A P.)—Japan has put to death some of the eight American flyers captured after the bombing of Tokio and, treating the others as criminals, is denying them the rights to which prisoners of war are entitled.

...

Green Presents State Budget; Cites 15 Million Spending Cut

BY GEORGE TAGGE

[Chicago Tribune Press Service.]

Springfield, Ill., April 21.—Gov. Dwight H. Green today presented Illinois' war model budget at a joint session of the senate and house and pointed in his message to reductions ...

Chicago Rate $10.42

8-DAY MORATORIUM SET ON EVICTIONS AS MAY 1 MOVING NEARS

...

REPORT NAZIS TO USE POISON GAS

Britain Warns of Full Retaliation.

LONDON, April 21 [Thursday] (A·P)—The British government in an extraordinary announcement said today that it had received reports that "Hitler is making preparations for using poison gas against the Russian front." It warned that such a development would lead the British retaliating with the same weapon and threaten the whole expanse of Germany.

...

Arnold Calls on Air Forces to Hit Back

Washington, D. C., April 21 (A·P)—Gen. Henry H. Arnold called upon his American air forces tonight to rest and to redouble their efforts to ...

ILLINOIS HOUSE G.O.P. OPPOSES WILLKIE IN 1944

[Chicago Tribune Press Service.]

Springfield, Ill., April 21.—The ...

THE WEATHER

TEMPERATURES IN CHICAGO.

...

Send for Good Surplus.

IN COLOR tomorrow!

TINY TIM'S VACATION GUIDE FOR BOYS

How young patriots this summer can help to win the war by having Tiny Tim alert to the dangers in a full page in color in tomorrow's Chicago Tribune. Don't miss it!

Front page of the Chicago Daily Tribune, Thursday, April 22, 1943. STAN COHEN COLLECTION

To

MARCINE

FLORENCE

PORTIA

CLEO

CONTENTS

FOREWORD

It was my good fortune to lead and to serve with many fine young men in the military service. Those who flew with me on the raid on Japan in April, 1942, have a special place in my heart and memory. They all volunteered for the mission knowing there would be a considerable risk. They were outstandingly skillful and courageous—truly superior.

Fortune served us well and circumstances allowed us to bomb our targets and escape. However, since the Navy task force was detected and it was necessary for us to leave the carrier earlier than we had planned, we arrived over China in darkness. Headwinds slowed us down and when we got near our destination, bad weather forced most of us to take to our parachutes or crash land. One plane, without permission, landed in Russia and the crew was interned.

Eight of the eighty men in our group fell into Japanese hands. When I arrived at a friendly Chinese headquarters, I tried every means at my disposal to get those men back. A large ransom was offered. The Chinese attempted to send troops in to rescue them. But the Japanese had suffered a severe psychological blow because of the raid and their eight captives were prize prisoners. No amount of money could buy their release; there were not enough Chinese troops available to take them back by force.

When I returned to the States, I kept trying to establish contact with these men through military, diplomatic and International Red Cross channels but without success. I was sent to other theaters of war during the ensuing months. Our Government continued to endeavor to learn of their condition and their whereabouts as the war progressed.

We were all deeply shocked when we learned that the Japanese had executed three of them for participating in the raid. They had been accused of "crimes" they did not commit. They were tried and sentenced to death under a law that had been enacted after their capture and for their detriment.

The five men who were not executed were given "special treatment," which meant a near starvation diet and solitary confinement for most of the period of their captivity. One of these died of beri-beri. The remaining four suffered greatly but finally came home after being liberated by American troops in August, 1945.

The story of these airmen is told here in full. The purpose is not to open old wounds nor to condemn the Japanese. Rather it is told so that we will all remember what evils an uncontrolled militaristic government can bring to its people and to point up what the consequences can be of our own unpreparedness to meet aggression. It is also a tribute to those courageous men who gave their all for their country. May it be a source of inspiration and hope for any who are now or who may become captives of another enemy in another armed conflict.

J. H. DOOLITTLE
General, USAF (Ret.)

PREFACE

In 1945, four emaciated American airmen were released from a Japanese prison in Peking, China. Their release made immediate headlines around the world and their poignant story answered a riddle that had mystified the Air Force since their disappearance forty months before.

These men were the surviving members of two B-25 crews that had followed the famous Jimmy Doolittle on his epic raid to Japan. Although they told their stories briefly after their release, they did not want to elaborate because they wanted to forget their experiences and pick up the pieces of their lives as best they could.

In 1962, I was privileged to attend the 20th reunion of Jimmy Doolittle and his Tokyo Raiders and begin research for a documentary of that famous air action. That book, entitled *Doolittle's Tokyo Raiders*, appeared in 1964 and did much to set the record straight in regard to the planning for the mission, the preparations, the fate of each crew and the strange aftermath. But while I was researching I saw another story that could not be told then because the men were not yet ready to tell it. It was the full account of the four survivors who had outwitted their captors and outlasted more than three years of brutal captivity.

After the war in Vietnam became serious, the experiences of these men and the lessons they had learned took on a special significance. When it was suggested that their story might be an inspiration to others who may find themselves prisoners in a foreign country, they each responded enthusiastically. The result is this book, which certainly could not have been written without their help and the encouragement of their wives and families. General Jimmy Doolittle not only supported the effort but also provided much "inside" information which only he could furnish.

I also wish to acknowledge the unusual assistance I received from Mr. and Mrs. Charles H. Towns, who had kept up an unceasing effort all through the war to find out the whereabouts of George Barr, in whom they had a special interest, and of his fellow raiders whose fate was also unknown.

Others who provided information include Dr. C. Hoyt Watson, former president of Seattle Pacific College; Dr. Stephen D. Sturton, the physician at Fengtai Prison in Shanghai; Dr. Fontaine G. Jarman, a paramedic who jumped into Peking; Colonel C. J. Krause, OSS team chief; Private Richard Hamada, member of the OSS team who located the survivors; Hilaire du Berrier, survivor of Fengtai; Admiral W. Scott Cunningham, who played an important role in the release of the fliers; and Major General William R. Peers, former OSS chief in Burma.

CARROLL V. GLINES

INTRODUCTION

Light rain pelted Technical Sergeant Nestor Jacot in the face as he tapped out a coded message on the portable high frequency radio transmitter in Peking. Beside him Staff Sergeant Dick Hamada vigorously turned the hand crank on the power generator. Around these two Americans stood a ring of Japanese gendarmes watching the operation stoically.

"We're getting through to Hsian now," Jacot said, patting his head set. "Now I'll send the good news."

The message Jacot then sent to OSS headquarters indeed was good news and made headlines around the world that day:

> FOUR DOOLITTLE FLIERS LOCATED IN MILITARY PRISON PEKING. NAMES ARE
> LT. GEORGE BARR, LT. ROBERT HITE, LT. CHASE NIELSEN AND CORPORAL
> JACOB DE SHAZER. BARR IN POOR CONDITION. OTHERS WEAK. WILL
> EVACUATE THESE MEN FIRST. ADVISE ETA OF AIRCRAFT.

The word traveled fast from Hsian to Kunming to Chungking. American war correspondents immediately flashed the story to the world that four missing members of Doolittle's Tokyo Raiders had been found alive. It was August 20, 1945, and the story pushed news of the Japanese surrender preparations off the front pages in the United States.

There was good reason why the release of these particular four Americans out of the hundreds who had been captured in the Far East should make headlines. These four had followed the incomparable Jimmy Doolittle on his epic B-25 raid on Japan on April 18, 1942. That single air strike, coming at a time when the Japanese were advancing steadily across the Pacific, had lifted the gloom that had descended upon America and her Allies. Doolittle's eighty men had performed a miracle by bombing an enemy capital city at a time when the nation's morale had reached the lowest point in history.

Of the eighty men who had flown the sixteen Mitchell bombers from the *Hornet's* decks, five of them landed safely in Russian territory but were promptly interned. The other seventy-five, their planes out of gas, either parachuted into the darkness over China or crash-landed along the beaches. Three of those men died. Eight others were captured by Japanese troops. The rest eventually made their way to safety.

When Jacot flashed his message from Peking, it was the first time that the fate of any of the captured men was known. Four of those eight had died a needless death. The remaining four, near death from starvation, could not have lasted another month.

The pages that follow tell the story of the eight captives. It is a story of torture and hardship, cruelty and persecution. It is also a saga of fortitude and faith, of courage and determination. It is told for the first time as a reminder of man's inhumanity to man and as a tribute to General Jimmy Doolittle and the gallant men who followed him on that day that made air history.

1
. . . . .

"TAKE ONLY VOLUNTEERS!"

WHEN COL. WILLIAM R. Peers completed his tour in Burma, he thought he might be going home. He had been responsible for all clandestine OSS operations in Burma until the deactivation of Detachment 101 in July, 1945. Instead of going back to the States, however, he had been ordered to China to assist Col. Dick Heppner, commanding officer of Detachment 202 which had been operating behind the enemy lines in the vast expanses of Japanese-occupied China.

The tall, slim Peers was put in charge of the area south of the Yangzte River and left immediately to take over his new command. Four weeks later he received an urgent message from Heppner: REPORT KUNMING IMMEDIATELY. URGENT.

Peers had not slept for 48 hours when he plumped down the metal steps of the battle-weary C-47 and saluted his boss. Heppner got to the point without any preliminaries. "Bill," he said, "the Japanese are going to surrender soon. General Wedemeyer has asked us to send rescue teams into Japanese Prisoner of War camps and get American POW's out of their hands before they can do anything to them. I want you to plan the operation. You have *carte blanche* to do whatever is necessary to get the job done. Prepare for the worst and take only volunteers."

Peers looked at his superior quizzically. "How much time have I got?" he asked.

"Forty-eight hours. The Japs are putting out peace feelers now. The problem is that we have no way of knowing what their reactions will be in regard to their prisoners. For all we know, they may take all POW's they hold and shoot them in retaliation for losing the war. Your job is to prevent that!"

Peers nodded and went to work. During the next two days working around the clock, he organized and planned the rescue operations centered around teams of five or six men each. He screened all agents available and organized four teams to be dropped into Mukden, Peking, Weihsien, and Shanghai. A fifth team was organized in Chungking to go into Seoul, Korea. These men were chosen from over a hundred seasoned OSS veterans who had been highly trained and had successfully operated behind enemy lines for months without detection. Some had parachuted directly into Japanese strongholds in the dead of the night. Others, disguised as Chinese and taking advantage of a long-established Chinese spy network, walked right through the Japanese lines. Still others, some of Oriental descent, successfully bluffed their way into the enemy-held coastal cities. One Hawaian-born Nisei had even arranged to have himself "commissioned" a Japanese captain, armed himself with fictitious orders and made "routine" inspections of every Japanese camp in his area of penetration. The agents' job this time, however, was to jump right into the middle of the largest Japanese strongholds in broad daylight and demand they surrender their prisoners. They were to use all their persuasive talents to convince the Japanese that any resistance to their efforts to release the prisoners would be useless.

When the men were ready to go, Peers delegated the task to several sub-detachments including one located at Hsian, China, under the command of Lt. Col. Gus J. Krause, veteran China-Burma-India cloak-and-dagger expert. Krause had anticipated the order many weeks before by sending a three-man team to the walled city of Peking. Weeks had gone by without a single word from the trio and then a single cryptic message was received. They had located a large POW camp with several hundred prisoners at Fengtai, four and a half miles southwest of the ancient city but had learned that more Americans were being held in the military jail inside the city. They were to go into Peking to check the rumor out.

The OSS trio did successfully penetrate the city walls but were unable to get out. They were incommunicado and virtual prisoners for three months in the enemy-held city, although they had not been detected. Each time they tried to leave the city their escape route was blocked by Japanese sentries who had been alerted to be on the lookout for three American spies.

The details of who these three men were, how they eventually escaped from a city teeming with thousands of armed Japanese and how they obtained the information must remain a secret even now. Suffice it to say that three brave men were able to report to their superior on August 6, 1945, that American prisoners were confined in "Prison #1407." Their report, code-named simply "Magpie Mission," gave the size of the cells, the furnishings in each cell, and the daily routine of the prisoners.

One by one, other teams had made similar reports on other camps to Gus Krause and he had forwarded them to Kunming. Krause and his staff knew that the day would come when this information might be useful. Time would be important to any rescue teams once they could get into the area where the POW camps were located. In view of the desperate nature of the Japanese militarists, it was quite possible that die-hard prison guards might try to exact a final vengeance on all American prisoners in the name of their Emperor. Peers was well aware of this and drove himself to the point of exhaustion planning all details of the mission.

On August 12, 1954, three days after the second atomic bomb had been dropped on Nagasaki, Dr. (Lt.) Fontaine G. Jarman and several other OSS men were playing cards in the OSS Officers' Club Room in Kunming. They were interrupted by the Detachment Adjutant.

"The colonel wants all officers in the mess hall at 2300 hours for an important announcement," he said.

The room buzzed with speculation but the card games did not stop. Each man looked at his watch and noted that he could play a few more hands before straggling over to the mess hall to hear what the Old Man had to say. Most of these men were seasoned veterans. A few, like Dr. Jarman, had been in the CBI theater only a few months. But all were of that unique breed of men who choose to serve their country anonymously and at great personal risk deep inside the enemy camp to whom the threat of death becomes a way of life.

On the dot of eleven, Col. Peers strode briskly to the front of the mess hall and addressed his men. "Gents, we've just gotten the word from Washington that the Japanese Government has decided to accept the surrender terms under the Potsdam Declaration," he told his men solemnly. "The war will soon be over. I want volunteers for special missions to liberate prisoners of war."

The tough, lean colonel, who would one day be in charge of the Army's Special Forces, outlined his plans briskly. "I'm not kidding when I say I want volunteers," he said. "This will be no 'cream puff' mission. You'll all be jumping in the midst of thousands of Japs who are armed to the teeth. For all we know they may not accept the commands of their headquarters in Tokyo to quit fighting. You have only one mission: get our men out of jail and back home. Anything else is secondary."

"Doc" Jarman was one of the first to volunteer. He was a physician who had been through parachute jump school at Ft. Benning. No one had to tell him that his job would be to check each prisoner's physical condition and render emergency medical care. He would assign priority to the most serious cases and see that they were evacuated by air as soon as planes could land safely.

Peers had decided on teams of five or six men to be headed by a field grade officer and to include a doctor, two interpreters, and a radio operator. Jarman was assigned to the team headed by Major Ray A. Nichol, a tall, handsome Alabaman. Also on the team were Lt. Mahlon Perkins; Sgt. Richard Hamada, interpreter; Pvt. Nestor Jacot, radio operator; and Pvt. Melvin Richter. They were originally assigned to fly to Mukden, China, but the distance was too great without refueling. It would have meant a one-way flight in which the plane, a B-24, would have had to be abandoned and allowed to crash. Instead, Nichol and his team were assigned to Peking. "Doc" Jarman recounts the incredible adventure that followed:

"We were briefed that the team of three OSS men, one officer and two enlisted men, had been in the area of Peking, and when last heard from, some three months previously, had relayed information that the Japanese were holding many American prisoners in a POW camp outside of Peking. They had reported that Colonel Devereux, the senior Marine Officer and Commander W. S. Cunningham, commander of Wake Island, were still alive and probably located in a heavily guarded prison inside the city.

"We flew from Kunming to Chungking and then Hsian on August 13th. At noon, on the 17th, the six of us were loaded aboard a B-24 which had the belly turret removed. Our destination was a small Japanese fighter strip outside Peking—a five-hour flight.

"The weather was perfect—hot, sunny and beautiful. We arrived over Peking fully expecting to be met by swarms of Kamikaze fighters foresworn to knock us down and make the supreme sacrifice doing so. There were no other planes in the air. We circled the city slowly while the B-24 crew members threw thousands of leaflets out which told the Japanese that the war was over and they were not to harm the American troops that were coming to accept their surrender.

"When the last leaflet was gone, the pilot circled the airfield where we were supposed to make our jump. The idea of the jump didn't scare me because I had qualified as a paratrooper in the States. But I was surprised to learn that Major Nichol was the only other member of our party who had ever jumped before and he had exactly one jump to his credit.

"We made one pass over the field and I sat in the opening where the belly turret had been, my feet dangling in the slipstream. Down below I could see hundreds of Jap soldiers scurrying to take up positions around the field. We were low enough so that I could see they were all armed with rifles and pistols. As far as I know, none fired at the plane. I was praying that they had all gotten the word to quit but I had no way of knowing and it worried me to see them all running with no indication that they intended to give up their weapons and surrender."

Jarman jumped on the next pass of the B-24 over the field. Below was a short concrete runway and he planned his jump to miss this and land in the grassy area. As soon as he pulled the ripcord, he looked down. There wasn't a sign of a single Japanese soldier. The field looked deserted except for several fighter planes parked on the landing strip. It gave Jarman an eerie feeling. He knew he was being watched by hundreds of pairs of eyes. What an easy target he would make, he thought, standing in the middle of a big field.

The same uneasy thoughts were going through the minds of the other Americans as they followed Jarman out the belly turret opening. One by one they landed in a line across the field, tumbled and then got to their feet. They unhooked their chute harnesses and gathered in the yards and yards of silk. Dr. Jarman describes the events which followed:

"I got out of my harness and started walking slowly across the field toward what looked like an administration building about 600 yards away. I looked back and saw that the others in my party had all landed safely so I thought that if we walked forward singly that we would present smaller targets than if we all gathered in a group. The plane circled once more, dropped our equipment and supplies then departed. An almost overwhelming feeling of desolation swept over me as the B-24 faded away.

"The equipment I carried seemed like a strange assortment for such a mission but actually it all had a purpose. I had three pistols, a carton of cigarettes, a pair of swimming trunks, and $10,000 in American cash. Each of us had the same amount except for Major Nichol who carried $50,000.

"Each of us also carried a letter from General A. C. Wedemeyer, commanding general of U.S. Forces in the Far East, addressed to the Japanese and saying, in firm words, that no harm was to come to us and that we were representing him until American forces arrived in strength to take over the city. Only one thing bothered me. The letter was written in English.

"I had walked about 100 yards when a burst of small arms fire split the air. I froze as bullets flew over my head sounding like a swarm of angry bees.

"There wasn't anything I could do. If they were aiming at me, they had missed. There was no place to hide and no place to run. I still couldn't see anyone to fire at so I decided they were trying to scare us and let us know that they hadn't given up yet. The firing finally stopped so I kept on walking as if I wasn't scared but I must admit I was. I fully expected to be mowed down in the next few seconds. If that was what they intended to do, there wasn't anything I could do about it.

"In the distance I heard a motor and saw a truck coming onto the field bearing a white flag. It steered straight for me at high speed and I thought they intended to run me down. It would be a strange way to die, I thought.

"The truck roared up and stopped in front of me. A Japanese lieutenant and three soldiers armed with rifles and bayonets surrounded me. The officer spoke a few words in English so I explained to him that I was not in charge of the American party, but that Major Nichol, several hundred yards to my right, would discuss our mission with him.

"I don't know what was going through the Jap officer's mind but after a minute's hesitation, he ordered the soldiers to pick up my equipment and put it in the truck. They then picked up the other members of my party and took us to their headquarters building."

Major Ray Nichol was the perfect man for the strange task before him. Tall, dark and an impressive bear of a man, he took charge of the situation as soon as he confronted the commanding officer of the field. Knowing that the Japanese were looking for the first sign of weakness in any discussions, he maintained a stern authoritative demeanor.

"I am Major Nichol, United States Army," he announced to the group of Japanese officers. "I wish to speak to your commanding general as soon as possible."

There were two Japanese intelligence officers present in civilian clothes who spoke perfect Oxford English. They had both lived in the United States and had actually been in the United States on Pearl Harbor Day. They had been repatriated along with other Japanese in an exchange during the spring of 1942.

The commanding officer of the field placed several telephone calls and summoned the Swiss Consul in Peking and Lieutenant General Takahashi, senior commander of Japanese troops in the area. After an hour of uneasy tension, Takahashi and the Swiss Consul arrived. Nichol got to the point after saluting courteously.

"General, I have been sent here by General Wedemeyer to arrange for the release of Allied prisoners of war," he declared. "We know you have a number of them, including the men captured at Wake Island. I want them released immediately."

Takahashi was nervous and perturbed at the effrontery of the American towering over him. "Major, I think your commanding general is premature in sending you here," he said through an interpreter. "The war is not officially over. Only a few high-ranking Japanese officers know that peace negotiations are underway. You are in extreme danger coming here like this!"

The Swiss Consul, seeing that he should assume the role of mediator, explained hurriedly that technically the general was right but that the Americans were not asking him to surrender. Their mission was a humanitarian one.

"Tell the General," Nichol interjected, "that I have a letter here from General Wedemeyer which tells him exactly why we are here. Tell him also that *he* will be in extreme danger if harm comes to any of *us*."

Takahashi was agitated and insisted that he could not control all the elements of his forces. It would help the situation, he said, if Nichol and his men would surrender their weapons since he could not guarantee their safety.

"Tell the General that we will not surrender our weapons and we are not asking him to surrender his—yet," he told the translators. "We want quarters for ourselves and we want him to start releasing the prisoners at Fengtai. I will not accept any delays or stalling around!"

After an hour of discussion with many side conferences being held by the Japanese, the six Americans were taken to the Grand Hotel des Wagon Lits, one of the two best hotels in Peking. They were interned there, mainly because Takahashi insisted that if they wandered around the city fully armed, some of his dedicated troops would think they would be honored by the Emperor himself if they killed the conquering Americans.

Nichol agreed to remain in the hotel where he had many talks with Takahashi. After many hours of discussion with no action on Takahashi's part, Nichol announced on the afternoon of August 19 that he and his men were going to leave the hotel regardless of the danger and visit the prisoners of war. Takahashi, seeing that he could stall no longer, finally agreed to release the prisoners that day. The first truckload was taken to the two major hotels. It included about 300 British, French, Australian prisoners, a few Americans, several hundred Allied civilians, and several Marine and Air Force pilots who had been apprehended by the Japanese a few days before hostilities had ceased. All were suffering from malnutrition, dysentery, and assorted illnesses, including malaria.

By the early morning of the 20th, all POW's at the Fengtai prison had been released. Nichol invited the ranking members of the camp to sit in on his next meeting with Takahashi scheduled to begin at ten o'clock that morning. By this time, Nichol had been well briefed by the ex-prisoners on the cruelty and tortures they had suffered during their imprisonment in Shanghai and Nanking before being brought to Peking. He knew the names of those who had died from tortures. When Takahashi arrived the room was electric with excitement.

Hilaire du Berrier, an American civilian who had flown for the Spanish Loyalists and later for Chiang, had joined a French Resistance Group spy network operating in Shanghai after Pearl Harbor. He had been captured and had survived almost three years in prison. He vividly describes the confrontation between Nichol and Takahashi that day:

"There were about fifteen Japanese officers present, including the commander of the Fengtai prison camp, Colonel Odera and Lieutenant Hondo, his interpreter. The meeting began pleasantly enough with Major Nichol obviously in charge of the affair. He was magnificently self-controlled as he exchanged pleasantries in the cultured Oriental manner. He talked about the weather, the excellent facilities in the hotel and how pleased he was that the Fengtai prisoners had been released.

"The general and the other officers, their huge samurai swords clanking against their chairs, were ill at ease but began to relax as Nichol smiled and continued to converse amiably.

"Then, without warning, Nichol's mood changed and he asked a direct question. 'General, I know exactly how many prisoners were moved from Nanking to Fengtai. Two of them did not arrive. What happened to them?'

"When the question was translated, the Japanese stiffened and the interpreter, Lieutenant Hondo, quickly answered for his superiors that they had died. 'But,' he added quickly, 'we have kept their ashes for you.'

"Hondo was visibly shaken by the question and his personal answer had confirmed a suspicion that Nichol had about him. Nichol glared at the lieutenant who shifted nervously and then sat down in a chair.

"Nichol shouted at him in a voice so commanding that everyone jumped. 'You will *not* sit down!' he exclaimed. 'I know now that you are not an officer in the Japanese Army. You are an interrogator for the Gendarmerie. Therefore, you will interpret but you will not have the privilege of volunteering information in this meeting.'

"Hondo jumped up as if he had been kicked, his hands shaking. After this exchange, Nichol lapsed back into talking about trivial things until the Japanese relaxed again. As soon as they had leaned back in their chairs, Nichol suddenly changed his mood and shot another question that shattered the atmosphere like a thunderbolt.

"'What happened to the man named Hutton?' Nichol asked. Hutton had died from tortures on August 15, 1944. Colonel Odera, sensing now that Nichol knew more than they realized, answered truthfully that he had died. Nichol asked about other men and then lapsed back into his pleasant mood again.

"The room was hot and Nichol was fanning himself with a Chinese fan. His manner was the coolest of anyone I have ever seen. The Japanese were weakening as the room got hotter and Nichol calmly fanned himself.

"Commander Cunningham, the naval commander of Wake Island when it fell, was observing the proceedings and thought that it was an opportune time for Nichol to mention that he knew that four of Doolittle's Tokyo Raiders were in the Military Prison in the city. He passed the information to Nichol who then demanded that Takahashi release the Doolittle fliers being held in special confinement immediately.

"The Japanese were obviously stunned. Apparently they had believed that no one but themselves knew they were in Peking. Without blinking, Nichol stared at the Japanese general and waited for an answer. No one moved. The general nervously unbuttoned his collar and squirmed in his chair. Nichol waited patiently for a reply and then made a striking gesture that spoke more than words. He carefully folded the fan he had been using and handed it to the general. Takahashi reached for it and began to fan himself. The gesture was, for that moment, the superb *touche*! Takahashi knew that this American was truly the master of the situation. He promptly ordered an aide to arrange the release of the men."

Within an hour the four emaciated Doolittle fliers were taken from their cells and began the long journey back from forty months of hell. Pvt. Nestor Jacot, the OSS team's radio operator, immediately flashed the word to Gus Krause in Hsian.

A few hours later the world knew for the first time the fate of two of Doolittle's B-25 crews who had gone down in enemy territory after the Tokyo Raid. For the first time, the world learned the tremendous psychological blow that the Doolittle raid had been to the Japanese. They also learned that the wrath and frustration of the Japanese people at the invasion of their homeland by sixteen American bombers had been directed toward eight airmen. Four of the eight had paid the supreme penalty and would never return. The remaining four, sustained by their faith and fortitude, had barely survived to document the cruelty and torture they had suffered.

2

"THIS FORCE IS BOUND FOR TOKYO!"

During the morning of April 1, 1942, twenty-two B-25 Mitchell medium bombers roared down the runway at McClellan Field near Sacramento, California. A few minutes later they landed at the Naval Air Station at Alameda and sixteen of them were towed to the pier where the U.S. Navy's newest aircraft carrier, the U.S.S. *Hornet*, was readying for sea. Giant cranes plucked them upward and set them down gently on the carrier's flight deck. Navy personnel chocked their wheels and lashed them down. That afternoon, a peppery Army Lieutenant Colonel who answered to the name Jimmy Doolittle, came aboard with 69 other officers and 130 enlisted men of the Army Air Forces.

At exactly 1018 the next morning, the *Hornet* hauled up its anchor and inched its way toward the Pacific in a thick fog. Behind trailed two cruisers, an oiler, and four destroyers. By 1148, the eight ships, designated Task Force 16.2, were in formation and plowing westward.

Once his crews had settled into their routine, Captain Marc A. Mitscher, the Task Force Commander, sent for Jimmy Doolittle. "Jimmy, for morale purposes," he said, "I'd like to tell this force where we're going. What do you think?"

Doolittle grinned at the leathery-faced Mitscher and replied, "I agree. I think some of my gang have already guessed but it's time your men knew."

Mitscher nodded and grabbed the mike for the ship's loudspeaker system. "Now hear this! Now hear this! This is the Captain speaking. This ship will carry the Army bombers on our decks to the coast of Japan for the bombing of Tokyo!"

The ship's complement of 2,000 men was silent for a moment, then broke into loud cheers. At the same time, the message was blinkered to the other seven ships that "this force is bound for Tokyo!" In the *Hornet*'s Action Report, Mitscher wrote that as a result of the announcement, "morale reached a new high."

Mitscher's report never reached the American people for it was classified "Secret" for over two decades. Although his crew's morale may have hit a "new high," national morale had reached a new low, for there was no darker period in America's history than that spring of 1942. The first four months of World War II, beginning with "the unprovoked and dastardly attack" on Pearl Harbor, had been marked by a series of Japanese military victories that had plunged the democratic nations of the world into deep gloom. In early January, 1942, the defensive structure of the Allies had crumpled everywhere west of the Hawaiian Islands and north of Australia. The Pacific Ocean had become a Japanese lake and the nation that the western world had not taken seriously was suddenly recognized as a major world power whose military strength and capacity exceeded every intelligence estimate. With surprising ease, thousands of square miles of territory had come under the Japanese flag. There seemed to be no limit to the spread of Nipponese aggression.

The first assessments of the damage caused by the Japanese attack on Pearl Harbor were a stunning blow to American morale, and the subsequent defeats at Wake Island and the Philippines were humiliating. But instead of panic and fear, the national reaction became one of fury and fight. Before in the nation's history, its people had rallied to slogans such as "Remember the Alamo!" and "Remember the Maine!" By the morning of December 8, 1941, a new slogan expressed the resolve of a nation that had never known defeat: "Remember Pearl Harbor!"

In the days and weeks following the "day of infamy," General George C. Marshall, Army Chief of Staff; General Henry H. "Hap" Arnold, Chief of the Army Air Forces; and Admiral Ernest J. King, Chief of Naval Operations, shouldered the unprecedented burden of responsibility for directing the buildup of the most powerful military forces in history. They were in constant touch with President Roosevelt in the White House. At each face-to-face meeting, the President always wanted to know when it might be possible to strike back at the Japanese by air just as the enemy had done at Pearl Harbor. He knew it would never be easy but he asked Marshall, Arnold, and King to keep their respective planning staffs thinking about ways and means of carrying out offensive strikes and retaliate for the humiliation suffered at the hands of the Japanese. To Roosevelt, some evidence of military strength was desperately needed to bolster public morale, which was sinking lower and lower every day as more and more bad news poured in from the Pacific.

Fortunately for the American nation, the gloom of defeat has always provided the necessary incentive for some creative thinking. Following a White House meeting in early January, 1942, "Hap" Arnold considered a suggestion by Admiral King that

Army and Navy fighters and Army bombers might be transported by carrier for possible Allied landings in North Africa. In his notes of the meeting, Arnold wondered what kind of bomber could take off from a carrier deck and memoed his staff:

"We will have to try bomber take-offs from carriers. It has never been done before but we must try out and check on how long it takes."

Only a week later another officer, Capt. Francis S. Low, a submariner on Admiral King's staff, watched some Army B-25's make simulated bombing passes at the outline of a carrier painted on a Navy landing field near Norfolk and had a flash of inspiration. He, like Arnold, wondered about the possibility of taking Army medium bombers off a carrier deck. But he also wondered if the bombers might be launched against the heart of Japan from carriers, in response to the President's continuing pleas for some offensive action in the Pacific. Low approached Admiral King, who referred him to Captain Donald B. "Wu" Duncan, his air operations officer. After five days of intensive study, Duncan reported that one plane, the relatively new North American B-25 medium bomber, was the only plane that could meet the requirements of such a mission as Low had suggested.

On January 17, 1942, Low and Duncan met with Hap Arnold. The boldness of Low's plan appealed to this airman of extraordinary vision and his reaction was enthusiastic; he did not disclose the fact that he had already considered the idea in connection with an invasion of North Africa. But he would need someone to check Duncan's figures—someone who knew airplanes as an engineer as well as a pilot, and someone who, if the idea was feasible, would be able to inspire the men who would fly the planes. He sent for Jimmy Doolittle.

Doolittle was not only a famous racing pilot and scorer of such aviation "firsts" as the first blind flight completely on instruments and the first outside loop; he also held a Doctor of Science degree in Aeronautical Engineering from M.I.T. and had spent a successful decade in civilian business after serving for thirteen years as an Army pilot. In July 1940 he returned to the Army and since January 1942 had been part of Arnold's staff to work on "special projects."

Without giving any details, Arnold asked Doolittle one question. "Jim, what airplane have we got that will get off in five hundred feet with a two-thousand-pound bomb load and fly two thousand miles non-stop?"

Doolittle pondered a moment before answering. "General, it'll take a little figuring," he said. "I'll have the answer for you tomorrow."

The next day, Doolittle reported that either the Douglas B-23 or the North American B-25 could meet Arnold's specifications—provided they were modified to carry more gas.

"Jim, there's one more fact I didn't give you," Arnold countered. "The plane must also take off from a narrow area not over 75 feet wide."

"Then there's only one answer, General," Doolittle replied. "The wing span on the '23' is too wide. The choice narrows down to the B-25. Now, why did you ask me?"

Arnold's smile widened. He quickly explained the basic idea and his enthusiasm was contagious. Doolittle immediately volunteered to take the project over, as Arnold knew he would. The broad plan was worked out between King and Arnold and relayed to their project officers, Duncan and Doolittle. The Navy was to get the B-25's within striking distance of Japan. The rest of the mission was Doolittle's problem. The best time for the raid from the standpoint of weather was before the end of April. That meant only three months to accomplish the thousands of details involved.

The fact that the concepts for the first joint Navy-Air Force operation in American history had such an informal beginning actually helped achieve the secrecy that was so vital to the success of the operation. By mutual agreement between Admiral King and General Arnold, the mission was to be treated as Top Secret with a minimum of records to be kept and as few people as possible knowing any of the details. Not only was the element of surprise absolutely necessary to achieve the desired psychological effect on the Japanese but the lives of over ten thousand Navy personnel and the safety of their ships would be involved. Both were irreplaceable at a time when they represented the only major offensive Allied military capability in the Pacific.

Since the type of aircraft had already been decided, the training of the crews would center around the plane and its capabilities. Doolittle decided that the men should all be volunteers and should be men with the most experience and skill at their respective jobs. The choice of the type of airplane actually determined the unit from which the men would be chosen. The B-25 was just entering the Air Force inventory. The only units with any real experience with it were the three squadrons of the 17th Bomb Group—the 34th, 37th and 95th—and the 89th Reconnaissance Squadron, stationed at Pendleton, Oregon but scheduled to transfer to Columbia, South Carolina. Almost all of their crews had flown submarine patrol off the Oregon-Washington coast.

Doolittle met with Lt. Col. William C. Mills and Major John A. Hilger, commander of the 17th Bomb Group and 89th Reconnaissance Squadron respectively, and outlined his requirements briefly after their arrival at Columbia. He asked them to pass the word to their men that volunteers were needed for an extremely hazardous mission which would require the highest degree of skill and be of great benefit to the war effort.

Stressing secrecy at all costs, Doolittle told Mills and Hilger that training would be conducted at an auxiliary field near Eglin Field, Florida and departure would be from a West Coast port around the first of April.

Every man who heard about the request for volunteers immediately called, wired or wrote to their commanders asking to be included. Hilger, a quiet, lean Texan, was the ranking volunteer so Doolittle immediately made him his executive officer. "You will be responsible for things at Eglin in my absence," he told him. "I'll do all the 'front-running' for you. Get things moving as fast as you can. I want 24 B-25's and enough men for 24 crews plus enough mechanics, armorers, radio men and other ground support people to get the planes modified and in the air for training. See you at Eglin."

The details worked out in Doolittle's mind were slowly taking shape. He planned to have the carrier bring his planes within 400–500 statute miles of Japan and bomb military and industrial targets in the Tokyo-Yokohama, Nagoya and Osaka-Kobe areas. After dropping their bombs, they were to proceed to five fields in eastern China for refueling and then fly to Chungking. The greatest non-stop distance involved was 2,000 miles.

Eighteen planes were to be taken on the raid originally, then it was decided that there was deck space for only sixteen. Each plane would carry its normal complement of five crew members—pilot, co-pilot, bombardier-navigator, radio operator and gunner-mechanic.

The best strategy, as Doolittle saw it, would be to plan on bombing the targets by daylight for greater accuracy. He thought a night take-off from the carrier best with arrival over Japan at dawn. If the chances were too much against survival in daylight, a night raid was contemplated. Upon arrival in China, rapid refueling would be required at the intermediate fields, before proceeding to Chungking. This meant gasoline had to be pre-positioned. Non-directional radio beacons had to be set up at the five fields. Ironically, because the Chinese could not be trusted to maintain secrecy, these arrangements had to be made without telling anyone in China the details or the "why" of any arrangements requested. As Doolittle wrote in his planning notes, shortly before the airplanes arrive, the proper Chinese agencies should be advised that the airplanes are coming soon but the inference will be that they are flying up from the south in order to stage a raid on Japan from which they plan to return to the same base." He added that "a premature notification would be fatal to the project."

Early in the planning phase, Doolittle hoped that negotiations could be made with the Russians to accept delivery of the B-25's as part of the lend-lease program. If the State Department could convince Moscow that this was a good idea, Doolittle could make delivery of his planes in Vladivostok after the raid. The problem would be greatly simplified because the distance to be flown would be shorter and there would be no need for involving the Chinese or having to make any arrangements for servicing or radio aids. But the Russians would have none of this. Accepting the planes after a raid on Japan would make them, in Japanese eyes, a party to the act of war. Fighting for their lives on the western front, they did not want to risk a war in the east with the rampaging Japanese. Doolittle had to eliminate this possibility completely from his planning.

Major Hilger and the major contingent for the "Special B-25 Project" arrived at Eglin between February 27 and March 3. Only Hilger knew any details about the project and rumors spread through the rank and file. He continually cautioned his men to talk to no one outside of their detachment.

Speculation among the pilots was heightened when Lt. Henry L. Miller, a flying instructor at the Pensacola Naval Air Station, reported for duty with the unit. Hilger had suggested to Doolittle before leaving Columbia that if they were to take off from a carrier, perhaps a naval aviator experienced in carrier take-offs should teach them how. "Good idea," Doolittle replied. "I'll see Hap about it."

Miller's job was to check out several of the most experienced men in the proper procedures for maximum performance takeoffs. He had never flown a B-25 before but the principles were the same for any airplane. He first instructed Captains "Ski" York, Davey Jones and Ross Greening from the co-pilot's seat until they were proficient and then the other pilots, including Doolittle and Hilger. Miller kept a running score for all 24 pilots. Only the most proficient of these were to go on the mission, although it was understood from the beginning that all 24 crews would go aboard the carrier. "This was for two reasons," Doolittle told the author. "No word could leak out from the disappointed crews if they were on the carrier and we would have plenty of spare crew members if anyone had to drop out at the last minute."

While the pilots were going ahead with their take-off training navigators made as many overwater and cross-country flights as they could. Gunners and bombardiers were scheduled for gunnery and bombing missions, but more often than not they had to cancel out because planes were not available, bomb racks were not ready, or guns would not fire. In fact, difficulties continued to plague those responsible for getting the planes ready for the raid—difficulties in installing the extra gas tanks necessary, difficulties with the planes' armament, even with the secret Norden bombsight until it was replaced by a simple sight costing only twenty cents to manufacture.

The crews trained with furious intensity during the brief time allotted to them at Eglin. While they were training Doolittle shuttled back and forth between Washington, Wright Field, and Eglin. He went through Lt. Miller's course in between trips and selected his crew. While in Washington he arranged for target folders, maps and intelligence information to be prepared. At the same time he followed up on arrangements being made in China to receive his planes, now scheduled to arrive on the night of 19–20 April.

The end of the training in Florida was sudden. Captain "Wu" Duncan had flown to Honolulu during the third week that the Doolittle detachment was at Eglin. He had made arrangements with Admiral Nimitz for a sixteen-ship task force centered around the carriers *Hornet* and *Enterprise*. In addition, two submarines, the *Thresher* and the *Trout*, were to scout ahead of the force and relay information on the weather and enemy ship movements. Duncan wired Low to "tell Jimmy to get on his horse." This pre-arranged signal was relayed to Doolittle from General Arnold and the great adventure was begun. On March 23, twenty-two heavily loaded B-25's roared down the Eglin runway. Destination: Sacramento, California. Nine days later, all twenty-two crews loaded their duffle bags aboard the *Hornet* and watched sixteen of their planes lashed to her decks. On April 2, the *Hornet* and seven supporting ships slipped their moorings and passed under the Golden Gate Bridge.

The sixteen Mitchell bombers lashed to the *Hornet*'s deck strained and bucked against their restraining ropes as Mitscher's eight-ship force sliced through the towering waves. Once out of sight of land Doolittle got his men together and gave them a complete briefing on the plan of attack:

The eight-ship task force they were with, he told them, would be joined by another eight-ship force centered around the carrier *Enterprise* with Admiral William F. Halsey in command. The sixteen ships were to steam westward so as to arrive at a point about 450 miles off the coast of Japan on April 19th. About 1,000 miles out the oilers and destroyers would detach themselves while the larger ships would go on to the intended launch point. Doolittle would take off during the afternoon of the 19th with incendiary bombs and strike Tokyo at dusk, then race southwestward across the East China Sea to Chuchow and land in darkness.

The other planes, armed with three 500-lb. general purpose bombs and one 500-lb. incendiary cluster, were to follow three hours later and reach Japan after nightfall. The fires set by Doolittle would guide the planes to Tokyo, Yokohama, Osaka, and Nagoya. All would follow Doolittle's escape route to Chuchow and the other fields in eastern China.

Doolittle passed out target folders to the sixteen selected crews and let them pick their targets. Once chosen, pilots, navigators, and bombardiers memorized every detail. This information was supplemented by tips on topography, prominent landmarks, enemy fighter planes, and anti-aircraft batteries, as well as escape and evasion techniques should they come down in Japan or Japanese-held territory. In addition, all pilots received lectures on carrier operations; Commander Frank Akers gave refresher training to the navigators. Bombardiers and gunners were given gunnery practice firing at kites let out behind the *Hornet*. Lectures were given by Lt. T. R. "Doc" White, a physician who volunteered as a gunner on Lt. Don Smith's crew. He warned them that "night soil" is used for fertilizer in the Far East and therefore, "everything is tremendously infected with a very potent organism to which most Americans are not immune." "The tiniest cut or scratch," he told them, "can get a raging infection in it within a few hours and whatever you do, take every nick and scratch seriously, as if your life depended on it, because it will."

On the morning of April 13th, the two task forces merged at the 180th meridian. On the *Hornet*, the B-25's were checked over from morning to night by their crews. Generator failures, spark plug changes, hydraulic system troubles, gun difficulties and leaky gas tanks kept the B-25 mechanics and armorers scurrying back and forth between their planes and the *Hornet* maintenance shop below decks.

Doolittle briefed his men twice a day and emphasized the importance of taking care of every detail. He reviewed the routes, targets, and bombing techniques and gave them advice on their conduct should they become prisoners. "You are to bomb military targets only," he warned repeatedly, "and whatever you do, stay away from the Imperial Palace. It isn't worth a plane factory, a ship yard, or an oil refinery, so leave it alone. You are to look for, and aim at, military targets only. Bombing military targets is an act of strategic warfare but hitting the 'Temple of Heaven' or other non-military targets such as hospitals or schools would be interpreted as an inexcusably barbarian act. It could mean your life if you are captured."

The continued warning about the targets by their scrappy leader had a telling effect on the B-25 crews. What had prompted the warning the first time had been a conversation Doolittle had overheard in the ship's ward room after he had allowed the men to choose their target cities. The pilots going to Tokyo talked about cutting cards to see who would "get the Emperor's Palace." The Doolittle brand of fury was vented at that moment and became indelibly impressed on one and all, especially Lts. Bill Farrow and Dean Hallmark.

Farrow, a tall, gangling South Carolinian, was almost an exact opposite to the lumbering Hallmark, a Texan whose nickname was "Jungle Jim." Farrow's crew consisted of Lt. Bob Hite, co-pilot, Lt. George Barr, navigator; Sgt. Harold Spatz, engineer-gunner; and Cpl. Jacob DeShazer, bombardier. Hallmark had Lt. Bob Meder as his co-pilot, Lt. Chase Nielsen, navigator; Sgt. Donald Fitzmaurice, engineer-gunner; and Sgt. Bill Dieter, bombardier. These ten men, representing the diverse backgrounds of post-depression America, were also typical of the other crews. The officers generally had more education than the enlisted men and the cleavage between the two groups was clear and definite on the ground as military custom demanded. In the air, however, the requirement for teamwork welded them together. The coming mission, with all its inherent dangers, broke the time-honored barriers between officer and enlisted man as the *Hornet* plowed westward.

The tension mounted as the hours melted into days. April 5th had been Easter Sunday and more men than usual showed up for the traditional service on the *Hornet*. Jake DeShazer, the son of an Oregon minister, did not attend—a dereliction that was to haunt him for many months to come.

Strict radio silence was maintained as the sixteen ships of the Halsey task force plunged on hour after hour. Although each of the ten thousand men in the force hoped their presence was not known to the enemy, their hopes were in vain. Japanese radio monitors had heard "conversations" between the Mitscher and Halsey forces as early as April 10th. Admiral Yamamoto, the brilliant commander of the Imperial Combined Fleet, had deduced that an American carrier force was approaching Japan and would arrive within carrier plane striking distance on the 14th. He immediately assigned long-range patrol bombers to search eastward on an around-the-clock basis. Fighter planes were repositioned around the Tokyo area. The line of approximately fifty fishing trawlers stationed off shore as picket ships was alerted to report any enemy activities. The following Japanese account describes the reaction in Combined Fleet headquarters:

> "Under mounting tension, the Combined Fleet made accurate calculations. If the enemy fleet were to proceed westward, Tokyo would be attacked from the air around the 14th, because even if the carriers came at full speed they would have to approach within three hundred miles of the home islands in order to fly the planes they carried. However, our surveillance net was 700 nautical miles off shore and the enemy, in order to break through this net and penetrate 300 nautical miles inward, would require 15 or 16 hours, so it would be possible for us to attack the enemy at our leisure the day before he launched his planes."

But April 14th came and went without any further report of the American task force. While their ability to intercept deductions from coded messages was better than American intelligence then knew, there was one basic flaw in Japanese deductions. Yamamoto and his staff were thinking that the two or three carriers they believed were in the American task force contained only conventional single-engine Navy bombers and fighters. No one suspected that the *Hornet*'s deck was loaded with

U.S. Army medium bombers. "Even if we had known it," one Japanese intelligence officer said after the war, "we would not have believed that they were supposed to fly from the carrier's deck. That would have been impossible in our view at that time."

On the afternoon of April 15th, Halsey ordered the carriers and cruisers refueled. The destroyers and tankers then withdrew to await the larger ships after the bombers were launched. The *Hornet* and *Enterprise*, unhampered now by the slow speed of the tankers, increased speed to 20 knots for the dash toward the enemy homeland.

As the hours passed, the tension on board the *Hornet* increased. Although it was originally planned for the launching of the B-25's to take place on April 19th, the force would now arrive at the take-off point a whole day early—a fact not known in Washington or Chungking and never explained by the Navy to this day.

On the morning of the 17th, the B-25's were loaded with bombs and positioned on the deck for take-off. Armament crews loaded ammo cans and engines were run up and checked for the last time. Fuel tanks were topped off and final maintenance was performed. When the work was finally finished at dusk, the B-25 crews and their buddies who would not be going on the raid went below to resume their nightly card games. This night, however, the games didn't last long. The eighty men earmarked for destiny hit the sack early.

At 3:05 A.M., the radar aboard the "Big E" picked up a blip and a message was flashed to the other ships: TWO ENEMY SURFACE CRAFT REPORTED. All ships were ordered to turn right to avoid detection. At the same time the General Quarters alarm was sounded and all hands rushed to battle stations.

A half hour later, after the enemy blips had faded from the radar screen, the six-ship force resumed its westerly course. Search planes took off at dawn from the *Enterprise* and a combat air patrol was launched to guard the fleet. The weather, which had been gradually worsening, did not look promising. Rain squalls swept across the decks and the green sea began to rise in 30-foot crests. Gusty winds tore off the tops of the waves and drenched the deck crews.

At 5:58 A.M., Lt. O. B. Wiseman, pilot of an SBD *Dauntless*, reported that he had spotted an enemy patrol vessel 42 miles from the force and added cryptically, "Believed seen by enemy."

This time Halsey ordered the six ships to turn left to avoid detection. The question on his mind was on everyone's. Had Wiseman been sighted?

While radio operators monitored the enemy radio bands and no Japanese radio traffic was heard, the half dozen ships again turned westward. Every extra mile they could get would be one mile less for the bombers to go. They were 700 nautical miles from Japan—the absolute limit of the range of the B-25's without any margin of safety to make up for head winds or errors in navigation. At 7:38, lookouts on

The aft section of the *Hornet* flight deck several days before entering enemy waters. One of the destroyers in the sixteen-ship task force is seen beside the carrier. The tail of the sixteenth B-25 on the deck hung out over the water. US NAVY PHOTO

the *Hornet* spotted the masts of an enemy picket vessel twenty thousand yards away. A few minutes later the *Hornet*'s radio operator intercepted a Japanese message, which had originated close by. The moment of decision had come. At 8:00 A.M., Halsey flashed a message to Mitscher:

LAUNCH PLANES X TO COL DOOLITTLE AND GALLANT COMMAND GOOD LUCK AND GOD BLESS YOU.

On the *Hornet*, Doolittle had been on the bridge with Mitscher, waiting and wondering. When the message from Halsey came, he ran to his plane shouting to everyone he saw, "O.K., fellows, this is it! Let's go!" At the same time, the blood-chilling klaxon horn blasted and Mitscher's voice boomed: "Army pilots—man your planes!"

The next twenty minutes were a blur of activity as each of the eighty B-25 crewmen jammed his personal belongings in his B-4 bag and raced to his plane. The sixteen bombers were stacked crisscross in two rows of eight, their noses angled in toward the center line. Tails and outboard wing tips overhung the sea.

At 8:15, a Navy "donkey" swung Doolittle's plane around and lined it up with two lines running down the deck—one for the left wheel and the other for the nose wheel. Doolittle and his crew, consisting of Lts. Dick Cole and Hank Potter and Sgts. Fred Braemer and Paul Leonard, settled into their respective crew positions. Engines were started and "the Boss" ran through his check list. He signaled to the deck hands that he was ready.

The plane director, Lt. Edgar E. Osborne, swung his checkered flag in a circle faster and faster—the signal for Doolittle to advance his throttles. The B-25 bucked and strained as the engines roared wide open.

At Osborne's signal, the wheel chocks were yanked away by the plane handlers. Ahead on the deck, green water broke over the bow and drained aft as the deck lifted into the air. Osborne's flag went up just as the *Hornet* crested a huge wave and dipped downward. His "go" signal was perfectly timed as Doolittle let off the brakes and the B-25 snapped forward. The Mitchell clawed its way down the deck and lifted skyward as the deck also rose. Cheers broke out on each of the six ships as Doolittle pulled the wheels up, came around in a tight circle and passed over the *Hornet* to check his compass.

The log of the *Hornet* records that Doolittle was airborne at 8:20 A.M. ship time. For the next hour, the remaining planes took off one after another but the take-offs were not without their critical moments. One pilot forgot his flaps and the first few had so much back-stabilizer rolled in that they were airborne in a near-stall. After that, Lt. Hank Miller wrote "Stabilizer in neutral" on the blackboard. One plane suffered a cracked nose glass when it was rammed into the tail of the one ahead of it on the wildly pitching deck.

The navigator on the sixth plane, Lt. Chase J. Nielsen, described his reactions after he had gotten the signal to load up:

"With the *Hornet* going full speed ahead into a 25-knot wind, it was almost impossible for us to stay on our feet. I slid down the deck on my hands and knees pushing my gear ahead of me in the general direction of our B-25. Several sailors, seeing my plight, rushed to my aid and helped me along. Some of the crew were already there and the others were being helped as I was. We stowed our equipment aboard, checked our bombs and guns, topped off the gas tanks, waved goodbye to the men lining the decks and took our crew positions.

"Lt. Dean E. Hallmark, my Pilot, said, 'Chase, you find Tokyo for us. Bob Meder and I will fly your headings. Fitz (Sgt. Donald E. Fitzmaurice) will keep the fighters off our tail and Dieter (Sgt. William J. Dieter) will clobber the target when we get there. If anybody wants to back out we have plenty of guys aboard willing to change places and we have about five minutes.'

"We all smiled at Hallmark and gave him the thumbs up sign. We wouldn't have let anyone have our places for all the rice in the Far East.

"All systems checked out and both engines started without hesitation. 'The Green Hornet,' as we called her, was as ready as we were. We all watched the first five planes go without much difficulty so we knew we should make it off all right. Dean was a top-notch pilot and we trusted his judgment completely.

"As Dean revved the engines up on the launch officer's signal, I felt strangely confident. I tensed when the flag flashed downward and Dean let the brakes off but the take-off was perfect—even better than any we had practiced. "The Green Hornet" was a thoroughbred in every respect as we leveled off and headed for Japan.

The other planes followed "The Green Hornet" one by one. The Navy deck hands, slipping and sliding along the bucking deck, did a superb job of getting them all in position. When the time came for the last plane to be moved forward, a near-tragedy struck. It was Bill Farrow's plane, nicknamed "The Bat Out of Hell," that seemed earmarked for disaster from that moment on.

Six Navy deck handlers were holding down the nose wheel of Farrow's plane to steady it from the buffeting created by the wind as Farrow taxied forward into position behind the 15th plane piloted by Lt. Don Smith. Just as Smith revved up his engines, the men started to move away from Farrow's nose wheel. One of the six, Seaman Robert W. Wall, lost his footing on the slippery deck and the blast of Smith's prop wash blew him into Farrow's idling left propeller. There was nothing anyone could do. The prop chewed into Wall's left arm and tossed him aside in a bloody heap. His deck mates rushed to him and whisked him to sick bay where his arm was amputated a short time later.

The crew of the sixth plane is shown here before their last mission together. (L TO R) Lt. Chase J. Nielsen (navigator); Lt. Dean E. Hallmark (pilot); Sgt. Donald E. Fitzmaurice (engineer-gunner); Lt. Robert J. Meder (co-pilot); Sgt. William J. Dieter (bombardier). USAF PHOTO

The sight of the sailor lying in a pool of blood unnerved Farrow. He had watched helplessly out his left window at the whole episode and was sure the unfortunate sailor had been killed. His hands shook slightly as he went through his cockpit check with co-pilot Bob Hite. Behind him, George "Red" Barr, the navigator, watched nervously from his position in the "well" behind the pilots. Corporal Jake DeShazer at the bombardier's seat in the nose checked his safety belt and tensed for the take-off. Sgt. Harold Spatz in the rear compartment gunner's seat checked in by interphone. Before any of the five men could think further about the plight of the sailor, Farrow got the "go" signal and released his brakes.

Historians can reckon for all time that the precise moment of the beginning of the end of Japanese dreams of world conquest is a half hour after noon on April

18, 1942. For it was at that moment that Staff Sergeant Fred A. Braemer, Doolittle's bombardier, opened the B-25's bomb bay doors, adjusted the twenty-cent bomb sight, and drew a bead on a large factory. Seconds later all four bombs were gone and Doolittle headed for the rooftops of downtown Tokyo, amidst intense but inaccurate anti-aircraft fire.

The weather from the carrier to Japan had been in favor of the Americans. They had departed under a low ceiling and visibility had been limited. The Japanese patrol planes still searching for any signs of an American task force missed most of the B-25's streaking in from the east. One of the Japanese pilots, however, did report sighting a twin-engine plane flying in the opposite direction but did not identify the type of plane. His headquarters assumed that he had sighted one of his own squadron mates or had been mistaken in thinking that it was an American twin-engine plane. After all, it was common knowledge the world over that the American fleet did not have any twin-engined planes on its carriers.

A few miles off the coast of Japan, the clouds became scattered and then almost non-existent as the long line of B-25's broke into the bright sunlight one by one. Ten of the planes streaked toward the center of Tokyo as they made their landmarks and located their targets in the sprawling city. Travis Hoover, and Bob Gray in the second and third planes dropped their eggs on factories, a warehouse, a gas plant, and dock area. Captain Davey Jones hit oil storage tanks and a power plant. Ted Lawson in "The Ruptured Duck" blasted a factory to bits. Hallmark's "Green Hornet" laid four bombs square into a series of saw-toothed roofs indicating a steel mill. Captain "Ski" York, followed by "Doc" Watson and Dick Joyce made direct hits on a power station, gas plant, and a tank factory.

The flight of three planes led by Ross Greening headed for the Yokohama dock area. Greening's bombardier, Staff Sergeant William Birch, lined up his sight on a large refinery and watched it go up in a tower of flames. Lt. Bill Bower's plane clobbered the dock area as did the plane piloted by Lt. Edgar McElroy. McElroy's crew reported that two of their bombs had hit a merchant ship being converted into an aircraft carrier. His co-pilot, Lt. Dick Knobloch, said later that the enemy ship toppled over in its floating dry dock "like a toy boat in a bath tub."

The tenth plane to be assigned to Tokyo targets was piloted by Lt. Everett W. "Brick" Holstrom, whose gunner reported that their top turret was inoperative shortly after take-off. To add to their misery, their gas tanks leaked and their magnetic compass was way off. The net result was that they hit the coast of Japan south of Tokyo short of gas. Their only protection against enemy fighters was the single .30 caliber gun in the nose. Although he was fourth to leave the *Hornet*, Holstrom found himself going upstream against all the other bombers making their escape southward. Fighters that had been alerted by the arrival of the other planes were waiting for him. In the sky over Tokyo, he could see the ugly black bursts of flak lingering from the barrages directed at his squadron mates. A half dozen *Nate* fighters, determined to score a victory, pounced on the helpless Mitchell and began firing. Tracers looped over the cockpit and Holstrom expected his plane to be shattered under the onslaught. He had given previous instructions to his bombardier, Corporal Bob Stephens, to salvo the bombs if they were bounced by the fighters. Reluctantly, Stephens pulled the salvo handle and manned the pathetic single gun in the nose against the swarm of determined enemy planes. Fortunately, the B-25, shed of its 2,000-pound load, quickly outdistanced its pursuers as it, too, took the southward escape route.

South of Tokyo, three planes made landfall and scattered to attack targets in Kobe and Nagoya. Major Jack Hilger smashed an arsenal, an aircraft factory and a barracks. Don Smith's bombs blasted a steel works. Bill Farrow, in the last plane off the *Hornet*, decided to hit his secondary target in Nagoya instead of Osaka, the primary. His bombs smashed into an oil tank farm and an aircraft factory.

After releasing their bombs, each plane dove for the ground and hedge-hopped southward along the seacoast until they cleared the main island of Honshu, then headed west toward the bases in China. "Ski" York, however, estimated that his plane could never make it to China. Instead of the normal fuel consumption, his engines were burning half again as much. He decided to head for Vladivostok, only about 600 miles away. While the other planes were winging their way toward China, York and his crew landed safely at a Russian airfield. Their joy at being safely on the ground was short-lived. Their airplane was immediately confiscated and they were interned.*

Not a single plane was lost to enemy action over the target areas although most had been intercepted by enemy fighters and had encountered heavy flak barrages. Only Dick Joyce's ship had sustained a hit and it had not interfered with the plane's flying characteristics. In the melee with the enemy fighters, however, the crews of Watson, Joyce, and Greening believed they had accounted for a total of five of them, a fact the Japanese have never denied.

As the fifteen planes streaking toward China roared along at low level over the China Sea, the good weather they had over the target slowly disintegrated. The fluffy scattered white clouds gradually joined and darkened, then became a ceiling, which let down lower and lower. Rain splattered their windshields as they ran through squalls. Headwinds slowed them down as they bored through a cold front and the pilots

---

*Captain Edward J. York and his crew were, for all practical purposes, made prisoners of the Russians. They were kept under guard for the next thirteen months in European Russia and finally escaped into Iran.

went on instruments. The Mitchells roared toward the fields in China they hoped were waiting to receive them, but they could pick up no radio beacons from the fields, and the darkness and weather were closing in. Plowing blindly through the rain and clouds and getting low on gas, each pilot knew he would have to make a tough decision—perhaps the toughest he would ever make. Should he and his crew bail out or should he attempt a controlled crash landing along the beach—if he could find the beach.

Doolittle's crew and the men in ten other planes elected to bail out into the ugly blackness. One of them, Corporal Leland Faktor, either struck something on the plane as he left or bailed out too low. His body was found by Chinese peasants next morning.

Four pilots decided to crash-land their aircraft. One pilot, Lt. Ted Lawson and his co-pilot, Lt. Dean Davenport, were catapulted through the windshield, still strapped in their seats. Both sustained serious injuries. The crew captained by Dean Hallmark landed in the surf off a beach, seriously injuring Fitzmaurice and Dieter. The other two crews, skippered by Lt. Travis Hoover and Lt. Don Smith, were luckier. Hoover landed in a rice paddy while Smith made a perfect wheels-up landing in the surf. Not a man on these crews suffered a single scratch.

It took a day for Jimmy Doolittle to round up his own crew. He felt a little better when he knew his own men were safe but there were seventy-five other men scattered over hundreds of square miles of Chinese territory and he didn't know where any of them were. He made his way to a Chinese military headquarters and asked the commander to spread the word to keep a lookout for his crews that might be adrift in the China Sea or wandering through the mountains.

As the whereabouts of each crew became known, Doolittle kept score in Chungking. All crews were accounted for by May 1st except two. With the safety of seventy of the eighty men assured, Doolittle felt better but was determined to try to locate the missing two crews of pilots Dean Hallmark and Bill Farrow.

The Chinese learned that the two missing planes had gone down in occupied territory. Two men had been killed—the Chinese could not say who they were—and the others were in the hands of either Chinese guerrillas or the Japanese. Doolittle followed up each report closely and offered a reward for the return of the missing men or ransom if ransom was demanded. He also tried to persuade General Ku Cho-tung, Commander of Chinese forces at Shangjao, to take the Americans away from their captors by force but the Chinese would have none of this. Regretfully, Jimmy Doolittle, newly promoted from Lieutenant Colonel to Brigadier General, left China on May 5th not knowing the fate of the missing men. He returned to the States to receive the Medal of Honor from the President.

The fate of the two crews—or what was left of them—weighed heavily on Doolittle's mind. He felt the loss of these men deeply. Although he was quickly ordered to command other men in the skies over the other two Axis capitals and was destined to wear the three stars of a lieutenant general by the end of the war, he could not erase the thought that these missing men were probably undergoing brutal tortures from their Japanese captors. He did not know how right he was.

The crew of the sixteenth and last plane to leave the *Hornet* poses for the photographer the day before their takeoff. (L to R) Lt. George Barr (navigator); Lt. William G. Farrow (pilot); Sgt. Harold A. Spatz (engineer-gunner); Lt. Robert L. Hite (co-pilot); Cpl. Jacob DeShazer (bombardier). USAF PHOTO

3

. . . . .

The Last Flight
of "The Green Hornet"

*T*HE REACTION OF THE Japanese to this bold intrusion of their skies by American airpower was one of surprise at first and then deep humiliation. While Japanese propagandists sought to minimize the damage for homeland consumption, the effect on the morale of the military leaders was considerable. The humiliation turned to rage as orders went out to seek and find at any cost the crews of any American bombers who might have gone down in Japanese-controlled territory. Any Chinese who may have helped them in any way were to be executed on the spot. All Chinese villages were given strict instructions to surrender any American fliers found in their territory with the warning that "the very stones of your towns and villages will be crushed into dust if you disobey."

A quarter of a million Chinese peasants paid with their lives for the Doolittle raid as the vengeance-seeking Japanese regiments slashed their way through the Chinese countryside during the next three months. The brutal retaliation was described by Reverend Charles L. Meeus, a missionary of Belgian descent who had become a Chinese citizen. He had followed the trail of revenge several months later after the Japanese had withdrawn and estimated that there were 25,000 murdered Chinese in the few villages he visited. He found the wreckage of Lt. "Doc" Watson's plane in Ihwang, Kiangsi Province, and heard the story from the townspeople of what had happened when the Japanese had located it several days after the raid:

"They found the man who had given shelter to Lieutenant Watson. They wrapped him up in some blankets, poured the oil of the lamp on him and obliged his wife to set fire to the human torch. They threw hundreds of people to the bottom of their wells to drown there. They destroyed all the American missions in the vicinity; they desecrated the graves of all these missionaries; they destroyed the ancestor tablets in the various villages they went through. Cannibalism is the only horror they spared the Chinese people of Kiangsi."

Columns of Japanese troops, preceded by planes dropping ammunition and supplies, continued to search over hundreds of square miles of territory in Kiangsi and Chekiang provinces for the Americans. They found plenty of evidence that Americans had been there. "Little did the Doolittle men realize," Father Meeus commented, "that those same little gifts, which they gave their rescuers in grateful acknowledgment of their hospitality—the parachutes, gloves, nickels and dimes—would a few weeks later become the telltale evidence of their presence and lead to the torture and death of their friends."

It is difficult for the Occidental mind to understand the rage and indignation that spurred the Japanese into such a furious campaign of revenge. Fifty-three Japanese battalions were ordered "to thwart the enemy's plans to carry out further air raids on the homeland of Japan." The main objectives were the airfields at Chuchow, Lishui, and Yushan, the planned destinations for most of the Doolittle raiders. When they arrived, after stiff resistance from Chiang Kai Shek's forces, they forced four thousand Chinese coolies to dig huge trenches at right angles to the runways. The job was so thorough that Gen. Claire L. Chennault, leader of the famous "Flying Tigers," remarked later that "it was easier to build new fields than to restore the damage."

When the bloody three-month revenge campaign was over, the Japanese Expeditionary Force withdrew toward Hangchow and allowed Chiang's forces to reoccupy the area. The operation had no other clear purpose except murder and destruction to teach the Chinese the consequences of helping the Americans. More significant, it demonstrated the deep-seated anger that the Japanese militarists felt and the belief that they had indeed "lost face" until they could retaliate with a similar raid against the United States. As one Japanese citizen told the author, "the raid had a tremendous impact on our thinking, although no one ever admitted it openly. My people had always been taught to believe what the Emperor and his military advisors told us. It was a severe psychological shock when it was announced that we had been attacked after we had been told that such an attack was impossible. We began to realize that we were not invulnerable—that a divine wind could not protect us from American planes."

The wrath of the Japanese high command was felt by the lowest soldier in the back country of occupied China. Shortly after the word was flashed to the commander of Japanese forces along the Chinese coast, word filtered through their spy network that two American planes had come down in occupied territory. All units were ordered on alert and to make contact with Chinese guerrilla forces who owed allegiance only to the Government that had the upper hand at the moment. When the Japanese were in strength, the guerrillas would obey them in order to survive. As soon as the intruders would leave, the guerrillas would return to their old habits of living off their own people. When it came to a toss-up, however, they hated the Japanese and would help the Chiang military forces in expectation of future favors. When the word spread that the American fliers were down, it became a race between the guerrillas and the Japanese to see who could find them first. The reward offered by Doolittle made the effort worthwhile to the ragtag Chinese guerrillas. The wrath of their raging generals made it mandatory for the Japanese.

Meanwhile, the American fliers they sought had had a rough time of it. After bombing steel mills in Tokyo, Dean Hallmark used the same exit route from the target area as all but one of the other B-25's did. He approached the China coast about sixty miles north of Wenchow at dusk. It was raining, clouds were low, and forward visibility was extremely limited so he elected to stay under the clouds at about 100 feet altitude. With all tanks indicating empty, Chase Nielsen, in the navigator's well, estimated that the coast was still ten minutes ahead of them.

"We'll keep on your heading, Chase, until the engines quit," Hallmark announced over the interphone. "Then I'll ditch it straight ahead. Count off the minutes for us so we'll know how far we'll have to row after we hit. Everybody strap yourselves in and wait until the plane comes to a complete stop before getting out. Make sure you've got your Mae Wests on."

Nielsen and the other three men acknowledged and when his count reached four minutes to go, the left engine coughed from fuel starvation and then the right. Hallmark held the plane straight ahead as it smashed into the waves and partially submerged. Nielsen, located behind the pilots, had called Don Fitzmaurice in the rear compartment to make sure he was braced for the water landing. Bill Dieter, the bombardier, had elected to stay at his position in the nose. Nielsen describes what happened next:

"It was a fast and very hard landing. As the aircraft hit the water, I heard Dieter in the nose scream. I saw the water pour up over the nose and then all went black momentarily. I had hit the side of my head against the back of the co-pilot's seat and was knocked out for a few seconds. When I came to, I was standing in water up to my waist and I was bleeding from gashes on my head and arms. My nose hurt and I knew it was broken.

"The two pilots were gone and so was Dieter who had been in his seat in the plexiglass nose section. Not only was Dean Hallmark gone but so was his seat which had catapulted right through the windshield.

"The water began to pour in so I climbed up through the hole, inflated my Mae West and joined Bob Meder, the co-pilot, on top of the slowly submerging plane.

Dean came up right behind me. He had bad cuts on his knees but they didn't seem to bother him. Dieter was in the water and climbed up on the right engine nacelle, while Fitz came out the rear side window.

"Dean and Bob immediately took the life raft from its compartment on the top of the fuselage while I helped Fitz up on top of the right wing. I noticed that the left wing and engine had been completely torn off and the severity of our situation suddenly came home to me. Waves twelve to fifteen feet high towered above us and slapped us viciously; it was now dark and our plane was sinking rapidly. All of us were cut and bleeding and I could see that Dieter and Fitzmaurice were in very bad shape. Dieter was incoherent and evidently had been badly crushed on impact when the brittle plexiglass nose slammed into the water. Fitzmaurice had a deep hole in his forehead where he must have struck some protrusion in the rear compartment.

"To add to our troubles, just as Bob pulled the lanyard on the CO_2 cylinder to inflate the raft, the cord broke off flush with the cartridge. The only way the raft could be inflated now was to blow it up by hand pump.

"While Dean, Bob and I scrambled to locate the hand pump in the raft kit, Dieter slipped off the wing. Dean made a grab for him but missed. At the same moment, a huge wave washed the rest of us off the plane which now was completely underwater. Bob Meder, seeing Fitz's condition, grabbed him as he was washed away. Each of us yelled to try to locate each other in the dark but in a few minutes the voices of the others were soon out of range and I was alone.

"I couldn't do a thing but ride with the waves. From the tide time table studies I had made on the *Hornet* before take-off, I figured the tide had just started in so it was in our favor. It was now about 9 P.M. and we had flown over 12 hours.

"I half-swam and half-floated for what seemed like hours. Thousands of thoughts flashed through my mind. I thought about my family, the fellows back at Columbia, S.C., who didn't go on the raid, the wonderful Navy men who had brought us to the launch point and were probably now being chased by the whole Japanese Navy. I wondered where the crews of the other fifteen planes were and whether Jimmy Doolittle's first combat mission might have been his last. Where were the other guys on my crew now? I feared the worst might happen to Dieter and Fitzmaurice because they seemed to be badly hurt. Then I began to worry about whether my navigation had been accurate. Were we only a few miles off the coast of China or a couple of hundred? I prayed that I had been right but was overcome with swift doubt.

"Just as I had about convinced myself that we must have gone down in the middle of the China Sea, I ran into some fishing nets. They were suspended from floating bamboo poles but I was too weak to climb over them. But finding them was good for my morale because I knew if I couldn't make shore that sooner or later someone would come out to check the nets. I cut one of the floats off as insurance in case my Mae West deflated.

"Then a sickening thought struck me. Suppose they were Jap nets and not Chinese. After all, the Japs had occupied the coastal area of China. Now I felt I had to get to shore before daylight and hide so I could get my bearings and then try to make contact with friendly Chinese."

Nielsen swam with the waves and ran into more nets. His cuts and broken nose were burning fiercely from the salt water and his strength was dwindling fast. After about three hours in the water, he heard the sound of breakers splashing against the rocky shore. After what seemed like another hour, his feet touched bottom and he fought his way to the beach against an undertow that threatened to pull him under in spite of the buoyancy of the Mae West and the bamboo float. Using his last ounce of strength he managed to swim the last few feet and crawl up on the beach. Finally free of the grip of the sea, he rested a few minutes and then opened his medical kit to tend to his wounds.

The fear of being discovered by the Japanese caused Nielsen to seek shelter but as he sought a place to hide, he fell into a crevasse and was knocked unconscious. When he came to, it was daylight and the sky was clear. Perched on the edge of the crevasse above him, two vultures watched hopefully.

"I eased myself up where I could see," Nielsen recalled, "and looked down at the beach below. It was alive with Chinese fishermen readying their boats for the day. No one could see me because I had lucked into a perfect hiding place. I had come ashore on the southside of a cove which was about three miles across. The shoreline was rocky for about a half mile to the west and then receded into pine trees which covered a gentle slope. Farther west was a small village of about fifty houses. A number of small boats rocked gently at their moorings along the waterfront. My blood froze when I saw two Japanese motor launches with their tiny red 'meat ball' flags fluttering on the fantails.

"Surveying all this, I decided to work my way into the tree areas as soon as I could. I saw no sign of my crew, equipment or the plane. It was like a bad dream or a Hollywood movie where I was more a spectator than a principal."

Nielsen picked his way cautiously toward the tree area and flopped into the brush beside a cobblestone path leading into the village. From this vantage point he could see not only the path, but the village and the harbor but still not be seen himself. His most urgent physical need was for water and he was able to find a few swallows by draining the rain water from some bamboo tree leaves. Once his thirst was satisfied, he realized he was hungry, but there was nothing edible in sight. Nielsen's narrative continues:

"I saw six soldiers arrive on foot at the dock and assumed them to be Japanese. They were armed with rifles, swords and pistols to varying degrees. After about 15 minutes of what looked like much ado about nothing, they finally boarded one of the patrol boats, started its engine and pulled out into the cove. It continued to the south, rounded the point and disappeared from sight. The Chinese junkers were out and tending their fishing nets. Some were already on their way back in with their previous night's catch of fish.

"I heard a horse clomping on the cobblestone path and it seemed to be coming down the mountain trail. As it came nearer, I could hear talking and assumed the language was Japanese or Chinese since it was sort of sing-song. I was approximately 100 feet from the path and fairly well concealed, though I could look around through the foliage and rocks and see part of the trail. The sight was rather amusing as it was a real poor skinny horse with several grass baskets mounted on its back similar to a pack saddle. Three uniformed soldiers were also aboard it and two more following, each having a sort of yoke over his shoulder with a large grass basket hanging from either end by ropes. There was a small pig in one basket, several clucking chickens in another, several pieces of dry wood in the third and the fourth was covered. I assumed that they were going to market in the small fishing village. Their uniforms looked somewhat different than those worn by the soldiers that had boarded the patrol boat. The color was different and these soldiers wore wrap leggings instead of knee high leather boots. The caps were also different and they all had small white insignia on the front with a blue ball and what looked like a 10 or 12 point star surrounding the ball. From pictures I had seen of Japanese and Chinese uniforms, the Japs wore a five-pointed yellow or gold star on the front of their caps and this looked like a Chinese insignia.

"I knew I must be positively certain of which was which before I made a contact, if I made one, and if Japanese and Chinese troops were both in the same area I wondered what the set up was. Not being able to speak or understand either language was a definite disadvantage.

"These soldiers seemed happy enough and knowing the Japs had occupied this coastal area put many thoughts through my mind. If the Japs had control, why didn't the Chinese fight back? On the carrier we were told that the Japs, after taking over in parts of China, had organized the Chinese in a sort of puppet operation and controlled them through fear. This must be so in this case, I thought. I would just have to sweat it out for a while longer and see if I could figure it out. I was certain there was a Chinese guerrilla garrison in the vicinity if the information I received while on the carrier was correct. How I would find, contact, or approach it, was of great concern. Should I try to find my crew members or take off alone for the interior?

As these thoughts ran through my mind I saw the belabored horse and group arrive at the edge of the village. I could hear the squeal of a pig and see much hand waving between these soldiers and some of the village people that had gone out with yokes and baskets to meet them.

"I couldn't imagine what all was going on but I saw two soldiers and several Chinese villagers walk down to the beach about 1,000 feet around from the dock area and congregate around something that I hadn't noticed before, but what looked like two men lying on the beach with life preservers on.

"My heart sank as I thought that they might be two members of my crew. The group stayed there a few minutes and then returned to their original meeting place. I watched a while longer and the soldiers and horse, with baskets full, headed back over their old route. I watched until they had gone by and as they did I noticed the articles in their baskets and took a better look at them. The baskets were filled with fish now, articles that looked like small loaves of bread and one was full of charcoal. There were several five-gallon cans, white rice, a front quarter of what looked like aged beef, and a wet U.S. Air Force life preserver. After close scrutiny I decided these men were Chinese but I was not ready to contact them yet. I had to be sure.

"I left my vantage point and worked back around the slope to see if I could get nearer those objects on the beach. I reached a small rice paddy and crawled on hands and knees along the dike for about 300 feet. If I could crawl about 200 feet more through the sparsely vegetated sand dunes that were now between me and my objective, I would know what it was. I knew I must find out because if they were part of my crew and I got out of there I'd like to know. Beside that, they could be injured and require help. I had one sand dune to go and I'd be within 200 feet. I looked ahead, picked a path and started for the top. This dune was only about six feet high and from the top I could see the entire beach. I crawled slowly through the sparse foliage, keeping my eyes down as I was afraid of what I would witness when I did look up. I crawled on and could see the sand slope steeply down. I knew I was at the top.

"As I started to look up, I first saw a pair of black split-toed canvas rubber-soled shoes facing me. Above these shoes, a voice in pidgin English said, 'Stand up or me shoot!'

"I had no weapon and was sure I was a goner. I asked myself if I would have time to rush the body in the shoes. I might be able to overcome him, I thought, but all he would have to do would be to squeeze the trigger. I made the decision to stand up and see what my chances were. As I did I saw the smiling face and hard set slant eyes of an Oriental. The insignia on his cap was the same as that of the group with the horse. He had what looked like a real antiquated buffalo gun pointed right at my midriff and the bore in the end of the barrel looked like a 16-inch cannon.

"I stood petrified for what seemed hours and finally finding my voice said: 'You Japanese?' His first reflex was to tighten those slitted eyes even more. He then raised his cheek from the rifle stock, spat on the ground and said, 'Me China. You American? You Japanese?'

"All the while that big gun aimed at my stomach never moved. I answered, 'I American.' I guess I have dark enough complexion to be a Jap but no slant eyes. Really, I'm a black-haired Swede.

"I could see the bodies on the beach now that I was standing up and I knew right away they were the gunner, Fitzmaurice, and engineer Dieter of my crew. The soldier saw my look go past him so in his broken English said, 'They dead. Bury them after hour. You go with me.' He nudged me with his rifle barrel and pointed to the cobblestone trail that was evidently the only avenue for all types of overland traffic. I noticed as I walked along that he stayed about 20 feet behind me, rifle pointed and ready, also that he would look toward the dock and open cove every few steps. I remained silent and moved on and as we crossed the rice paddy dike, I could hear the throb of a boat engine entering the cove. At this he said, 'You run fast up path! Japs come! Will kill me, you.' I could have outrun him but didn't dare for fear he'd shoot.

"At any rate, when we were far enough to be screened by foliage, he said, 'You stop!' I stopped and he came up, slung his rifle over his shoulder and said, 'We fight Japs. You no worry now. We go see my chief. Talk all about you then. Go fast, follow me.'

"A million things were going through my mind and I had as many unanswered questions, but if I was getting away from the Japs I could afford to remain silent and hurry. We hiked up the trail for about an hour and finally came upon several small tile-roofed wooden buildings. In the center at the top of a pine pole, the Chinese Nationalist flag was fluttering. It was a welcome sight but as a military garrison a far cry from anything I had ever seen before.

"There seemed to be about 25 or 30 shabbily dressed soldiers in this garrison. Facilities were meager but the stench from human waste and rotten fish was outstanding. I was taken to a small panelled room and left. However, he did leave a pockmarked guard at the door and this one looked like one of the most wanted criminals. I was glad to sit down so I could get my mind straightened out. I could hear much talking down the corridor so tried to prepare myself for my fate and just sweat it out. After about 10 minutes my warden came back and escorted me to his chief."

The chief of the guerrilla band was a young, well-built, good-looking Chinese officer in a clean, tailored uniform. His manner was pleasant as he questioned Nielsen through the soldier-interpreter who had captured him. To questions about his mission, Nielsen was noncommittal, saying only that he was one of five American fliers who had dropped into the sea. His most earnest desire, he said, was to find the rest of his crew and get to Lishui, their assigned destination.

Nielsen was puzzled at the strange relationship between the Chinese and Japanese military forces. Both were well established in the area but apparently, as long as the Chinese minded their own business, the Japanese left them alone. A Japanese garrison of 150 soldiers was located about five miles away. Nielsen was told that the guerrillas would try to get him into "free" China but that every precaution had to be taken to prevent his being seen. If the Japanese found him travelling with them, every one of them would be shot on the spot.

The Chinese confirmed that two of his crew had been found dead on the beach and their bodies removed so the Japanese wouldn't find them. Coffins were being made and as soon as it was safe, they would be given a soldier's burial. Nielsen knew then that Dieter and Fitzmaurice had been as badly injured as he had feared when he saw them last.

The friendly interrogation was interrupted by an orderly bringing in a tray of food. During the meal word came that the Chinese had located another member of the crew and that he would be hidden until all was clear. In the meantime, word had gone out through the mysterious grapevine system to look for the fifth crew member, protect him from the Japanese and bring him to the village. At the same time, the Chinese started to plan to move the three men inland through the Japanese-controlled territory to freedom.

After the meal of boiled eggs and rice, sea weed soup and semi-cooked fish "that smelled like it had been dead for a month," Nielsen was allowed to look over the compound. Upon inquiring about latrine facilities, he discovered that a large wooden bucket was used and the contents went to fertilize the rice paddies. Urine was released anywhere and the most popular place was the patio in the center of the buildings. Nielsen noted with some misgivings that the drainage from this area was directly toward the compound well. In the barracks area, soldiers were washing their uniforms by merely wetting them and then beating them with large flat bricks.

While the soldiers appeared to be in good health as far as he could see, their yellow skin, deeply slanted black eyes and rough, pock-marked faces gave them an inscrutable sadistic look that made Nielsen's blood tingle. They eyed him from head to foot and then began to laugh. "I found out later that they were laughing at my size," Nielsen said. "I am only six feet tall, but I was a foot taller than any of them. I guess I was as amusing to them as they were to me."

That afternoon, Captain Ling, the officer-in-charge, and Chen, the interpreter, led Nielsen out of the compound over a rough back trail to the village. As they neared it, the stench of dead fish got stronger and almost overpowered the Utahan, who was having trouble making the noon meal stay down. They were met by an elderly Chinese wearing a small black skull cap, a long black robe and wooden clogs. He spoke briefly to Chen and motioned for them to follow him into one of the first four shanties along the cobblestone street.

Nielsen had an ominous feeling as he ducked inside a narrow doorway. It was dark but the light from the open door cast light on the body of a man stretched out on a pallet in the far corner. It was an elderly Chinese who appeared to be mummified with his skin drawn drum head tight over his fragile bones as if to crush them. As he stared, he sensed a motion behind the door and snapped around to see what it was. Instinctively, he threw up his arm and jumped aside. There stood the huge frame of "Jungle Jim" Hallmark, his pilot, with a big club above his head, ready to swing. Hallmark had thought the intruder was one of the Japanese patrols inspecting each house and taking no chances, was prepared to crush the skull of anyone who attempted to capture him.

The reunion of the two Americans was joyous as they quickly compared notes. Hallmark's knee was badly cut and he was bruised all over but he could walk. He had not seen any of the crew since he, too, had been washed off the top of the sinking plane. Nielsen told him about the fate of Dieter and Fitzmaurice. Ling and Chen led them back to the compound where they were joined by Bob Meder, the co-pilot. Meder told them how he had grabbed Fitzmaurice and swam all the way to the beach pulling him by his Mae West straps. Fitzmaurice became unconscious and by the time Meder dragged him up on the beach, the young engineer-gunner's life had ebbed away. A short time later he found Dieter's body. Apparently, Dieter had been able to swim most of the way in but could not survive the head injury he had also received. Meder dragged both of their bodies above the high tide line before he went into hiding.

The three survivors of the *Green Hornet* hid in the guerrilla garrison while the routine Jap patrols came through the village. So far, they did not know of the crashed B-25 and had not been alerted to look for it or for its crew. When the patrol left, Hallmark, Meder, and Nielsen were led to the place where the Chinese had hidden the bodies of Dieter and Fitzmaurice. They gently placed the bodies of their comrades in two wooden boxes, selected a point high up on the beach and buried them. The three officers prayed silently over the graves of the faithful enlisted men who had given their last full measure of devotion. These two, like Cpl. Leland Faktor on the crew of Lt. Bob Gray, had made the supreme sacrifice for participating in the bold raid on Japan.

Captain Ling and his interpreter, Chen, took the three Americans aboard a sampan crowded with Chinese soldiers and civilians the next morning. After sailing for a couple of hours, a Japanese patrol boat was sighted. Ling sent the trio scurrying below decks into a small dark compartment in the stern. The stench of bilge water and human excrement made them retch as they crawled beneath grass mats and rags and lay still. The Japs halted the sampan and a boarding party searched it from one end to the other. As the three of them lay there trying not to breathe and retch, the door to the compartment was pushed open and a soldier jammed a stick around in the darkness. Nielsen was poked viciously but did not cry out. Satisfied that they knew everything about what the boat carried, the boarding party left. just as the motor launch chugged away, Nielsen's stomach could hold back no more and he added his contribution to the bilge.

When darkness came, Ling ordered the sampan to anchor off a small village where the three Americans were put up for the night. Next day they anchored off the walled city of Wenchow while Captain Ling went ashore. He returned with the news that there were many Japanese sea and land patrols out searching for the Americans, who had bombed "the land of the dwarfs" as the Chinese referred to Japan. Therefore he could not take them any farther but had arranged to have them taken to the next city by others who could be trusted. They would stay that night in Wenchow, however. When it was dark, they were rowed ashore and led through the ancient wall and into the city past hundreds of small wooden, tin-roofed shacks. The Chinese they passed paid them no heed although their height and their facial features branded them as Occidentals — a rarity in that part of China.

They arrived at a building in the center of the city and went inside to meet an elderly white-haired Chinese named Wong. To their amazement, Wong spoke perfect Oxford English that he had learned while studying in England and at St. John's University in Shanghai. He had once been a Buddhist monk but now described himself as "a poor fisherman."

Ling left the trio in care of Chen and their newly found friend who served them a delicious dinner. Nielsen describes the events that followed:

"Sage Wong told us of the hardships the Japs had imposed and the sadistic way they treated the Chinese. How they had assaulted young Chinese girls until dead. How they beheaded the men and boys with their heavy swords and this was done with no restraint from the Jap officers because they were no better than the Jap soldier. I asked him why many of the Chinese guerrillas didn't fight the Japs and was surprised to hear him say that they were no better either. They both preyed on what little the Chinese civilian had until life was not worth living and he hoped his Buddha master would send for him soon.

"We didn't have long to talk because a young Chinese in his early teens came rushing in and talked very rapidly to Mr. Wong. He was really excited and from his action fear grasped my heart. I looked toward Chen and saw his hand reach for his rifle; his slitted eyes had all but closed and as he jumped for the doorway was met by two of his comrades. Mr. Wong waved the boy aside and looking us square in the face said, 'The Japanese soldiers are at the gate opening. They are starting to search this side of the city. We must move and hide from them if we can.'

"He told Chen and the other soldiers to stay there to avoid suspicion and if the Japs asked why they were there to make their own excuses. He would contact them after the Japs left. He rushed us out and down an alley toward the gate we had entered. He said he planned to get us to a boat if possible. He figured if he could get us to sea we would be more difficult to find amid the many boats anchored in the river mouth. He shoved us in another building and ran to see where the Japs were. On return he told us they were still progressing toward us. We moved on until we were at the Northeast gate and peering around the corner of a building I could see that avenue of escape was cut off. About a dozen Jap soldiers were there and ready to man machine guns already set up on tripods. Mr. Wong took one look and analyzing the situation called several Chinese and with us in the center and hidden by their long robes or kimonos, walked us across the 12-foot road in a group and into the east side area of buildings. We ran through another alley and were pushed into a building. Mr. Wong disappeared again but returned quickly. He said the Jap soldiers, about 30 of them, were making a thorough search of the entire walled-in area and progressing toward us and that we must try to hide where we were. He sent all the Chinese scampering away and the four of us were left alone.

"I looked all around but couldn't see any place that would possibly conceal three Americans. These buildings were all scantily furnished and this one looked more bare than the others had. We made a fast decision and Dean dove in a corner. Bob and I covered him with some grass mats, sacks and a couple of old blankets and shoved a make-shift bench in front of the pile. We both then climbed into the rafters in opposite corners as it was the only cover we could see. My heart was pounding wildly and I was really sick at heart. I wish we could have stayed on the sampan until we could transfer to the junk to go up river. This had been suggested but Captain Ling was against it, although he never said why. I wondered where he was now. Mr. Wong sat down on the floor and busied himself by attempting to light a charcoal fire in a metal container. It seemed like an eternity and my body ached from trying to roost on that small rafter and trying to squeeze into the darkness of the corner at the same time, but at last, as I had dreaded, the Jap soldiers came down the alley. I could hear their hob-nail soled boots on the stones and brick. One soldier stepped inside the door, looked at Mr. Wong who now wore a real poker face. He also looked about the room and his gaze stopped on the corner where Dean was. I wasn't sure if he really knew what he was looking for but at any rate he seemed to think it wasn't there. He turned and left. If he had listened he would have heard the trip hammering of my heart.

"As he left I sighed in relief, and prayed that soon they would all leave the area and not return, especially to that building. I could hear several soldiers still stomping around outside and was surprised to see Captain Ling enter followed by what looked to be a Japanese officer with two heavily armed Jap soldiers. Captain Ling addressed Mr. Wong and as he sort of shrugged his shoulders with his reply, Captain Ling reached out and slapped him real hard across the face. One Jap soldier backed into the doorway and drew his sub-machine gun to hip level. As he did this the other soldier approached the corner Dean was in. He kicked the bench out of the way and started kicking at the sacks and grass mats that covered Dean. I could have jumped on him but it would have cost me my life as the soldier in the doorway would have cut me in two with his weapon. About two more kicks and Dean was uncovered. The Jap officer, speaking in very good English said, 'You, you in the corner, stand up and walk out only two steps. If you don't, I'll have you shot immediately!' Dean reluctantly and slowly complied. As he did the Japanese officer grunted several commands to his troops. At this, more guns appeared, pointing in through the windows and more soldiers appeared at the doorway.

Captain Ling simply stood there, in front of the Japanese officer not saying nor doing anything. The Japanese officer then asked Dean, "Where are the other two men?"

Dean looked him straight in the eyes, took a long deep breath and answered that he didn't know what he was talking about and asked, "What other two men?"

"The Japanese then turned to Mr. Wong, pulled his pistol out and started yelling at and beating the old man. Wong fell to the floor and cowered against the wall nearest the corner below my perch. The Japanese officer then drew back and as he did his head tipped back and he stood staring right up at me. I don't know if Mr. Wong had told him where I was, but at that same time one of the soldiers just inside the door started to yell and point his sub-machine gun up at Bob. We were ordered to climb down and stand with hands up by the other American. I reluctantly complied.

"I was so sick I couldn't even think. I suppose I was thoroughly stupefied. I could hardly hear him when he said, 'You are now prisoner of Japanese. You have nothing to fear if you do as you're told. You will go with us now to our military camp.'

"I didn't have much time to think because an order had been given and the Japanese soldiers were beginning to tie us up. Our hands were pulled behind our backs and secured with handcuffs. A rope about six feet long was attached to the handcuffs and the other end tied into the belt of a Japanese soldier. I assumed this was to prevent us from attempting to run.

"While we were being tied the Japanese officer talked to Captain Ling who seemed to be putting up quite an argument. What it was all about I wasn't sure, but I think he might have been trying to keep us in his custody. The Chinese, even though under a puppet set-up, were still our allies. At any rate, after about three minutes of heated sing-song conversation, much waving of hands and pistols, the Japanese officer cocked his pistol and pointed it at Ling's chest. Ling took a long look at us, holstered his pistol, faced the Japanese officer, saluted, bowed and immediately left without uttering another word.

"Mr. Wong remained cowering in the corner where he had been knocked during his abuse by the Japanese officer.

"Upon receiving the word that we were securely tied, the Japanese officer said to us, 'We will go now to my superior officer. Do not try to escape or you will be shot and killed.' As we departed the building I heard someone yell 'Long live America and China, I hope they kill all the Japanese.' I was not sure who it was but assumed it to be Mr. Wong.

"Some of my senses started to function again as we headed up the road outside the walled area, toward what looked like a military garrison. I didn't pay much attention to the adjacent area as I was now deep in thought and wondered just how it was that the Japs had found out that we were there. Something didn't ring true about the whole set up. The search made by the Japs seemed to have been too organized. Also, it had seemed as though they knew what they were looking for. The Jap officer upon finding Dean had asked him where the other two men were so he had known there were three of us. Captain Ling, though a Japanese enemy, was our ally but it was evident that he had offered no resistance to the Japs other than orally. He wouldn't arm us with weapons when we had suggested it and it seemed that he had been foresighted with his diplomatic salute and bow when he departed. The summary of these thoughts led me to believe we had been sold out. Captain Ling could easily have planned for our capture with the Japs when he had gone alone into the city to arrange for our boat trip up the river. Instead it seemed that we were sold down the river. Also, he had insisted we go into the small walled area rather than stay on the sampan and transfer to the junk when it came.

"I couldn't help wonder about it all and knew I would never know the answers unless I asked. I started to talk to the Jap officer, who was now almost walking at my right side. At the sound of my first word I was jerked off my feet, by the soldier at the end of the rope attached to my bound hands, and I fell sprawling in front of him. As I lay there I saw a hobnailed boot traveling fast in the direction of my chest and as my hands were tied behind me all I could do was roll. This I did and the boot caught me in the side with terrific force. It all but knocked my breath away. I was then roughly jerked to my feet. Amid the laughs and smiles of the Jap soldiers, their officer told me I was not to talk until questioned by his superiors. So, I remained silent.

"Normally a procession of any kind would have created some interest for the general public but in this case I suppose the Chinese didn't dare chance a second glance because they gave way in front of us as though we were a new scourge sweeping their country. Besides the Jap officer (I assumed that he was an officer and the only one in this group, not only because he seemed to be in command but also because of his neat uniform and highly polished boots), there were about 32 soldiers. They were all dressed alike except for their rank insignia on their coat collars. Their uniforms were a light khaki color and made from what looked like rough cotton material. They all wore knee length hobnailed leather boots of a rough work type. All were heavily armed. The variety of weapons consisted of many potato-masher type hand grenades, swords, rifles, sub-machine guns, pistols and what looked like several water cooled machine guns with tripods and ammunition belts. The officer's uniform was somewhat darker in color, and looked to be of a wool fabric. On his head he wore a natty little cap to match. His boots, of the English riding style, were also brown in color and polished to a high shine but they were not hobnailed as were the soldiers'. White cloth gloves covered his hands and around his waist he wore a polished brown leather belt upon which hung his holstered pistol and the customary Samurai sword.

"At the moment he looked like the cat that ate the canary and I suppose he had reason to be rather proud of his catch, even though we three looked like the last of the Mohicans. My morale at this point was about two feet lower than a deep deep well. Our odds of 50-50 had all run out and it now looked like our chances of survival and return to our loved ones and the United States was about 1 to 99 if that much.

"With no further ado than the clumping and scraping of hobnailed boots on the brick road we proceeded northward for about a half mile when we were pulled to an abrupt stop in front of a large pair of wood gates posted with two Jap military sentries. Upon command from the Jap officer with us, one of the gates was opened and we were jerked, pushed and pulled inside.

"I immediately assumed this place to be a Japanese military garrison from what I could see. The roadway from the gate we had just entered, gave way to both the right and left joining about 100 yards straight ahead and making sort of a small circle. At the center of this circle stood a large wood flag pole, at the top of which a Japanese Rising Sun flag fluttered in the breeze.

"As the gate was closed behind us my heart really sank. It was the first complete feeling of actually being captured and at the mercy of the enemy that finally took a full hold on me. From stories I had heard of the sadistic treatment the Japs were capable of putting out, I had a real sick feeling that my future was perhaps going to be much shorter than I had planned thus far.

"Bob, Dean and I were led through the camp and many Jap soldiers started to appear from the buildings near us. I assumed they were barracks since most of them were three stories high and articles of washed military clothing were draped from the bottom of the windows. From their rough lumber structure, rusty tin roofs and the clothes in the windows, it reminded me of an oversized shanty town.

"Many of the soldiers fell in behind our procession and continued to follow until we were pushed inside the front door of what appeared to be their headquarters building. It looked like the war was over for us."

4

. . . . .

EARMARKED FOR DISASTER

THE "GREEN HORNET" had been airborne from the carrier about twenty minutes when Lt. William G. Farrow and his crew loaded their gear aboard. The last plane on the crowded deck, its fuselage hung out over the edge of the fantail and Sgt. Harold Spatz, the engineer-gunner, could not load through the rear hatch until the plane moved forward. Farrow started the engines and Bob Hite, his co-pilot, crawled in beside him. Corporal Jacob DeShazer, the bombardier, stuffed his equipment into the nose while Lt. George Barr strapped himself in and spread out his maps.

The *Hornet* was pitching wildly as the Navy deck handlers swarmed around each plane until it got the take-off signal. Green water splashed over the bow and ran down the flight deck as the carrier plowed at maximum speed through the thirty-foot waves. The sailors slipped and slid around Farrow's plane as they jockeyed it into position, behind the fifteenth plane piloted by Lt. Don Smith. Smith revved his engines up on signal, while Farrow idled his and wondered how the Navy deck handlers kept from getting hurt. At that moment six deck handlers were holding down on the nose wheel and started to move away when Seaman Robert W. Wall lost his balance and fell into Farrow's idling propeller. The prop chewed into Wall's left arm and threw him aside. His deck mates quickly rushed him below. A short time later, Wall's arm was amputated and he became the first casualty of the Tokyo Raid.

The sight of Wall's bloody form on the deck unnerved Farrow and his crew but there was no time to think. At exactly 9:20, one hour after Doolittle had departed, the last plane blasted skyward safely.

The first plane to take off from the *Hornet* was piloted by Lt. Col. James H. "Jimmy" Doolittle. Other planes followed in quick succession; the last plane, piloted by Lt. William G. Farrow, took off an hour after Doolittle's departure. US NAVY PHOTO

After dropping his bombs on an aircraft factory and an oil tank storage area, Farrow headed south and then west as he had planned to do. His plane was burning more gas than he had anticipated and his navigator, George Barr, kept continually at work estimating their ground speed as they sped along about 500 feet above the wave tops.

About 7:20 P.M., after running into the ever-increasing murky weather, Barr sighted a lighthouse on the China coast and advised Farrow to climb because of the mountains which reached upward into the clouds behind the beach. Farrow climbed the B-25 to 11,000 feet on instruments. Barr quickly gave an approximate heading to get them to Chuchow, their intermediate gas stop. After an hour of instrument flying, co-pilot Bob Hite tried to contact the ground station to get a radio bearing but there was nothing but static. He tried to tune in the radio DF station that they had been told would be broadcasting but, again, nothing.

"We're in a tough situation, fellas," Farrow announced to his crew over the interphone at 8:30 P.M. "We obviously can't find Chuchow in this stuff and I'm not going

A replica of the "Mark Twain" bomb sight constructed at Eglin Field to the specifications of Capt. C. R. Greening. Materials cost about twenty cents for each sight. Knowing airspeed and altitude, each bombardier could compute the angle at which the sighting bar should be set. When the target passed the line of sight, bombs were released. SIGHT CONSTRUCTED BY LT. COL. H. E. CROUCH; PHOTO BY F. N. SATTERLEE.

to try to let down underneath it because I'm sure these clouds are full of rocks. We know Free China is to the south and we know Chungking lies to the west but too far away for the gas we've got. I'm going to keep on heading southwest to see if we can run out of this weather and make a forced landing."

Barr, the navigator, disagreed with this plan of action. He recommended flying west for fifty minutes and then south to make sure they were out of Jap-infested territory and then bail out. But Farrow and Hite saw things differently. They were pilots and wanted to get the plane down in one piece, refuel and fly on to the destination at Chungking.

Barr was overruled but he understood how they felt. He tried to compute their probable position as they bored southwestward through the clouds. At about 11:45, the fuel warning lights came on. Simultaneously, there was a break in the clouds which revealed the lights of a small city. "That's Nanchang," Barr announced.

Before they had left the *Hornet*, they had been told that the area surrounding Nanchang was presumed to be in Japanese hands. But they had no choice. One by one the five men dropped into the blackness. Sgt. Harold Spatz went out the rear hatch. Corporal Jake DeShazer went out the hatch in the navigator's compartment, followed quickly by Barr, Hite and Farrow.

The day before the takeoff, the Doolittle crews witnessed Capt. Marc Mitscher, skipper of the *Hornet*, presenting medals for Lt. Col. Doolittle to attach to a bomb destined to be dropped on Tokyo. The medals had been presented to U.S. sailors years before by the Japanese during a goodwill visit to Japan. They requested the medals be returned to Japan "with interest." US Navy Photo

Each of the men landed safely although they were spread out over a line several miles long. Within several hours, however, Barr was captured by the Japanese. That night Hite, limping from a badly sprained ankle, was also captured and put in the same room with Barr. The next afternoon, Farrow, Spatz, and DeShazer were rounded up and the interrogations started immediately. Bob Hite described what happened:

"They took us into a room one at a time and asked us who we were and where we had come from. There was no doubt in their minds that we were Americans but, apparently, they didn't tie us in with the Tokyo bombing and it didn't seem at first that they even knew about it.

"Frankly, I was getting scared. They had handcuffed us even though we were kept in individual cells and put about four or five guards outside each door. They took us out one by one to a large room where about a dozen officers, all in full military

This unusual photo shows Lt. George Barr, navigator on the crew of Lt. William G. Farrow, smiling beside two of his Japanese captors. Photographed in Tokyo after being captured, Barr and his crewmates believed they would be treated humanely as prisoners of war. Barr had not yet been tortured when this photo was taken. He was smiling at a photographer who had fallen backwards while taking pictures of the captives. USAF PHOTO

A photo of Lt. Farrow and his crew was used on this poster as a warning to the Chinese. The inscription reads:

"Severe punishment will be given under military law for the outrageous and inexcusable attack by American airplanes upon the territory of the Empire.

"As a result of interrogation by the military legal office, each of the American pilots who were captured by us will be severely punished by the military law for their outrageous, inhumane, bestial and devilish crimes. Last April 18th they dared to attack the holy territory of the Empire and moreover directed their attack at non-military targets including hospitals, schools, and private homes, either dropping incendiary bombs or high explosives and even swooping down with machine guns strafing elementary school children at play."

Top row, left to right: Lt. William G. Farrow, Lt. George Barr and Lt. Robert L. Hite. Bottom row, left to right: Cpl. Jacob DeShazer, Sgt. Harold A. Spatz. USAF PHOTO

dress and obviously delighted with their prizes, questioned us through an interpreter. They told each of us we would be shot if we didn't answer all their questions.

"I guess all of us were a little cocky even though we were apprehensive. We knew we should only give them our names, ranks, and serial numbers, which we all did. But we each answered other questions and embellished the answers a little by trying to lead them off the track. George Barr and I told them we were pursuit pilots. George told them he had bailed out and hit his head and couldn't remember anything about his unit or his mission. He tried to act dazed but I don't think they were fooled.

"Although they were furious, our captors didn't do any more to us at that time except shove us around a little. Later that afternoon, after bringing us together and telling us that we would be shot if we tried to escape, we were loaded into a 1938 Ford truck and taken to an airport. We were led into a transport plane similar to our own DC-3 with a single row of seats along one side and a double row along the other. I got to thinking that this might be our chance to escape—that if Farrow or I could take over the controls of the plane, we could fly on to Chungking. There wasn't anything we could do, though. With four guards per man who jumped every time we moved and being blindfolded and handcuffed to the seats, we would have been dead men before we could ever get to the front of the airplane.

"We landed about an hour and twenty minutes later and were whisked to a jail in separate cars—all 1938 4-door Fords. There were guards on either side of us and two in the front seat. The drivers blew their horns incessantly, and since I have a big nose and could see under the blindfold, I saw coolies, donkeys, children and dogs scatter wildly as we plunged madly through the streets. It was Shanghai, a city we would soon see again.

"We were put in solitary cells and forced to sit cross-legged on the floor. I still had my heavy flight jacket on but I shivered uncontrollably—probably from the cold but also because I was hungry and, I guess, scared.

"About 9 P.M. the guards brought me a cheese sandwich made out of white bread and a cup of tea. It was delicious. When I finished I felt better but terribly exhausted. I lay down and promptly went to sleep.

"Shortly after midnight, two guards came in and yanked me to my feet. They led me down the hall, took my blindfold off and pushed and pulled me across a patio into a large building and up three flights of stairs. I was shoved into a room where a Japanese major, an interpreter and four guards were waiting. 'You will please to sit down,' the interpreter said, motioning to a chair in front of their table.

"'Do you care to smoke?' the interpreter asked as he shoved a box of White Owl cigars and a package of cigarettes toward me. I reached for the cigarettes with my two shackled hands. As I did, the cigarettes were withdrawn.

"'You may have them afterward,' I was told.

"'After what?' I asked naively.

"'After you tell us what we want to know.'

"'I am a prisoner of war,' I told them. 'I am not required to give any more than my name, rank and serial number which I have done.'

"'You will give us more!' the interpreter shouted suddenly. If you don't, we will have you shot where you sit!'

"I felt reasonably sure that the Japanese would treat us as prisoners of war and

Lt. Robert L. Hite is led blindfolded from a Japanese transport plane after being flown from China to Tokyo. Shortly afterward, Hite and the other seven Doolittle Raiders were tortured and beaten. USAF PHOTO

that the threats were just part of the act to scare the unwary. I decided they were bluffing and didn't know anything about us so I would only answer what I wanted to. I stared at the interpreter and he waited for the officer to say something.

"The officer, a stern-faced individual whose military bearing set him apart from the enlisted men, smiled and leaned forward. He had a pile of papers in front of him and he shoved them toward me. 'Look at this,' he said in perfect Oxford English.

"I leaned forward to look and saw that he had a complete roster of all eighty men who had gone on the raid.

Closeup view of five of the eight Raiders captured by the Japanese and flown to Tokyo for interrogation. (Rear row, l to r) Lt. William G. Farrow (pilot); Lt. George Barr (navigator); Lt. Robert L. Hite
(co-pilot). Front row: Cpl. Jacob DeShazer (bombardier); Sgt. Harold A. Spatz (engineer-gunner). Spatz
had been allowed to have a cigarette. USAF PHOTO

"'Do you know Doolittle?' he asked.

"'Yes, I've heard of him. He's an American stunt flier" I answered.

"'We want you to know we have captured him and his crew,' he announced flatly.

"I was stunned but then I remembered an old gangster movie.

This is what the police said to make a suspect talk. I couldn't help but smile. When the officer saw this, he started firing questions at me fast.

"'What does H-O-R-N-E-T spell?' he asked.

"I answered 'hornet.'

"'What is that?'

"'It's a bug—a kind of a wasp.

"'It's an aircraft carrier, too!' he said sharply.

"'I wouldn't know about that,' I told him. 'I am not familiar with the other branches of the service. I'm in the Army Air Corps.'

"'You are one of the men who bombed the Japanese homeland and we know Doolittle was your leader. Now, where did you come from?'

"'If you are an officer in the Japanese Army, you know I can't answer that,' I told him.

"The questioning continued and I gave him nothing but I could tell from his questions he already knew quite a bit about us. Since he kept asking where we came from, I finally decided to tell him. 'From the Aleutians,' I said, hoping that I made it sound convincing.

"The officer seemed elated and broke off the interrogation. I was taken back to my cell. Next morning, the five of us were blindfolded, taken to the airport and loaded aboard the same transport we had used the day before. We flew for a couple of hours, landed for fuel and tailwheel repairs and took off again.

"About two and a half hours later we started descending. I managed to sneak a look under my blindfold and saw that we were circling a body of water. I strained a little—and then I saw a big sprawling city. I knew instinctively what it was. We were landing at Tokyo!"

The five luckless members of Farrow's crew had indeed arrived in Tokyo. They were put in individual sedans and driven to a military barracks area where they were led into a building with rows of individual cells. Blindfolds were removed and each was placed in a separate cell still handcuffed. About an hour later they were stripped naked. Their clothing was searched, then returned minus ties and belts. They were taken to interrogating rooms where a pattern of torture and scientific persuasion began. There they were to learn a basic lesson for which the Japanese would later pay dearly: torturing and killing of prisoners of war would become commonplace under the Japanese. Thousands of Allied military and civilian prisoners would suffer starvation, mutilation and death before the fighting would cease. The captured Doolittle Raiders were to be the first Americans to experience the highly skilled torture methods of the dreaded Kempei Tai, the Japanese counterpart of the Nazi Gestapo.

Although Japanese Army and Navy units all used the same general torture methods, the Kempei Tai members were true professionals at the art of breaking down a prisoner mentally and physically. The Kempei Tai were the Japanese Army's Military Police, administered by the War Ministry. The men assigned to the headquarters unit in Tokyo were masters of the craft. Although the war against the United States was only six months old, these men had been perfecting their techniques for over a decade in their aggressive actions in Manchuria and against the Chinese.

Farrow and his crew immediately sensed the difference in the atmosphere as soon as they entered the interrogation rooms in Tokyo. Each room had a table and chair. As soon as a prisoner entered the room he was thrust into the chair. An officer, an interpreter and three or four guards were always present. The tempo of the questioning at first was always slow and then rapidly picked up as the questions were asked. Bob Hite described his first Tokyo grilling:

"They offered me a cigarette and when I reached for it they slapped my hands. There was a mean-faced guard standing in the corner who held a big stick. At intervals he would come charging at me shouting loud noises and brandishing the stick. He'd charge right up to me and then swing viciously at my head. At first I ducked but then I found he never followed through. He would stop his blow short and just tap my head gently. Obviously, he was trying to scare me but after he did this a few times, I just sat. In between times, the officer asked questions, the interpreter translated and I would either answer truthfully if it wasn't a military question like 'Who is the President of the United States' or make up some weird answer if I thought it wouldn't hurt our war effort in some way.

"When they finally led me away to my cell after this first encounter, I felt pretty good. If this was the 'first team,' they weren't so tough and the two hours they had tried to get something out of me were wasted as far as they were concerned. Little did I know that this was Step One in their progressive torture process."

Hite, Farrow, Barr and the others were more exhausted than they suspected after the first question session. They were led back to their cells and tried to lie down but the guards beat on their cell doors and yelled until they sat up and crossed their legs.

At about 9 P.M., the second questioning session began. This time each man had a different set of guards and officers, and had been led to the interrogation room with leg cuffs on and baskets over their heads. This time there was a Japanese civilian in the room who looked like a clerk since he wore the old-fashioned sleeve protectors and made frequent notes. He turned out to be an interpreter who spoke cultured English with many American colloquialisms. Since he prefaced every English sentence with "Well, well," he acquired this as a nickname.

The guards from this point on were tough specimens who never smiled or showed emotion of any kind. Well-Well started off the second sessions by telling the fliers that they didn't want to be rough on them. All the Americans had to do was cooperate and answer all questions.

The questions began innocently enough but soon got to the heart of the matter. Had they taken off from the *Hornet*? How long was the *Hornet*'s deck? How many bombs had they carried? Why had they said they had flown from the Aleutians or Midway, when it was known that the B-25 couldn't fly that far? How many airplanes were on the raid? How many men?

In each case, the first evasive answer brought vicious slaps across the face from the guards. The questions got more searching and the slappings got more severe. Well-Well would follow each slapping session with a short lecture on telling the truth and promised that the punishment would cease as soon as they decided to cooperate. He also promised other and better means of persuasion if they did not stop evading the truth.

Each of the five Americans did his best to resist the interrogations for which they were rewarded with slaps and punches to the head and body. After two hours of this they were led back to their cells sore and stiff with their ears ringing. Barr became deaf in one ear from a blow by a rifle butt.

The interrogations continued every two or three hours for several days. The five prisoners were fed watery rice and tea three times a day and could rest only when the guards weren't looking. As soon as the guards found them dozing in their sitting positions or toppled over, they would shout and jam long poles through the small window in the door. Slowly each man's will to resist was deadened as his body weakened from the poor diet and fatigue. The questioning sessions got rougher. The guards now kicked them in the groin and the shins and smashed their faces with their fists from behind when they refused to answer. Then the special tortures for which the Kempei Tai are famous began.

First was the water torture. The victim was bound or handcuffed with his hands behind him and forced to lie on his back on the floor. Guards would hold or sit on his legs. Another would sit on his stomach while another would pin the prisoner's head between his knees to keep his head facing upward. A towel was placed in cuplike fashion over the mouth and nose. A guard would then take a bucket of water and pour it into the towel until the victim lost consciousness. The result was literally like drowning and the Kempei Tai experts knew exactly how far they could go and still bring a person back to life. They would let the victim loose and apply pressure to his lungs, sometimes by jumping on his abdomen, to force the water out. After the coughing and sputtering stopped, the process was repeated several times until the victim grew so weak he lost all strength to resist the treatment. At this point, the torture would suddenly cease and the questioning resume.

Next came the knee spread. Each prisoner was forced to kneel with a bamboo pole, as much as three inches in diameter, inserted behind both knee joints so as to spread them. Pressure was then applied to the thighs, usually by jumping on them. The feeling, as George Barr later described it, was that "it seemed like my kneecaps were coming loose." Each time the guards jumped on their thighs, the pain was so intense that they almost blacked out. Then a strange numbness would set in as the blood circulation was shut off. The torturers knew when this occurred and would stop the jumping, jerk the victim to his feet and let go. Each man would crumple to the floor because all feeling and strength had gone. The interrogators would roar with laughter as their captives scrambled around on the floor trying to get to their feet.

Then came the finger torture. This was a simple but effective method where sharp sticks about the size of a pencil were jammed between each finger and into the membrane where the fingers joined. The fingers were then bandaged or tied together tightly. Then one torturer would squeeze the hand with all his might while another would slide the sticks back and forth. This method was as painful as the others and resulted in dislocated knuckles. At the least, the fingers were badly bruised and swollen for several days.

The results the Japanese wanted were obtained in some measure. In their anguish, each of the men would answer a question to make the torture stop and if the answer was a "right" answer, a nod from the officer would make the guards back off. Shortly, there would be a knock on the door and an interrogator and an interpreter would come in to share some tidbit of information he had gleaned from one of the other prisoners. There would be a whispered conversation and then a new line of questioning would start.

While most of the questions concerned the raid itself, their training, and the *Hornet*, some were intelligence questions about the United States in general, what the Americans thought about the Japanese, the war and President Roosevelt. Sometimes the questioning would center around certain cities and they would be asked about the industries there, the type of smoke coming out of chimneys and the location of railroad stations, airports and power stations. Although most of the men had never been to these cities, they tried to give answers that sounded plausible and logical. The only way they knew when they gave wrong answers was when they received a swift kick in the groin or were slugged from behind. In no case would the Japanese allow the helpless prisoners to say they had never visited the city or did not know the answer.

Farrow and his men were gradually being reduced to automatons from the interrogations. They were not allowed to wash or shave. Their matted beards and their body odors further added to the demoralizing process. Being in solitary confinement and incommunicado with the other crew members compounded their individual miseries. Each wondered what his personal fate would be and what had happened to the other Tokyo Raiders.

While Farrow and his crew were suffering in Tokyo, Hallmark, Meder and Nielsen had been flown to Shanghai on April 24. The three of them were given the same tortures as the others—water torture, knee spreading and finger laceration. But a new device and a new psychological twist designed to break a prisoner's will to resist interrogation were added. Chase Nielsen, tough, lean Utahan, describes his experience:

"I was dragged into a small room and placed on a table. Around this table there were winch-like devices on all sides. Leather straps were placed about my ankles and wrists and a collar was placed about my chin and the rear lower part of my head. I had heard or read of this device somewhere and how it had been used in the Middle Ages. It was a human stretcher.

"My legs and arms were all hooked up, the winches turned and finally I was pulled above the table and hung high and dry. After a short discussion between the officers the winch at my head was pulled real tight and I felt like my head was about to come off. I was really scared now. The wound in my left arm from the plane crash was really alive with piercing pain and I hoped that I either passed out or died real quick. I was sure I couldn't take this long, but was now more determined than ever that I'd die without telling them a thing.

"The collar about my chin and head was making it difficult to breathe and had cut off the circulation to my head but thanks to this I was released just prior to blacking out. I was taken out of harness and pushed into a chair and as the blood returned to my head and eyes and I could see and hear again, the interpreter told me that I was foolish to take any more punishment because my buddies had already talked and they knew the whole story.

"'Tell it to me and I'll see if it's right,' I said. The officer laughed.

"'Oh, no, you tell it to us,' he said and nodded at the enlisted men. The four bullies began to work me over even more thoroughly than before. One would twist my arms until I went to my knees, then I would be jerked to my feet and kicked in the shins. Every few seconds one of the soldiers would haul off and slap me hard and the Jap officer would laugh.

"'How do you like that?' the interpreter would ask. Then I would get another blow or a kick and he would say, 'How does that feel?' Then my arms would be twisted and he would ask in his monotone voice, 'Do you want to say anything now?'

"I didn't try to resist too much because I soon found out that the soldiers would only twist harder and that if I didn't resist the blows weren't quite as strong but I tried to fall away from the blows whenever I could and protect myself as much as possible. That went on for about a half hour. I was wet with sweat, very weak and boiling mad. If I could have got my hands on any kind of weapon I would have killed some of them, but, of course, I would have been killed too so it was probably better that I didn't.

"The Jap officers seemed to tire now. One of them spoke to the interpreter and he turned to me.

"'Well,' he said, bowing and smiling, 'if you insist on not telling us anything we might as well finish the job right away. You will face the firing squad for execution immediately.'

"One of the soldiers put my blindfold back on and I was led from the room.

"After they had tried the water torture, the bamboo treatment, the stretcher and plenty of beatings without getting any information from me, the interpreter announced in a voice laden with sorrow that they had decided to execute me only because I had refused to cooperate with them. He said it was a pity because my folks back home would never know what had happened to me.

"I was blindfolded and led from the room in Shanghai's airport prison by two soldiers. Outside the sun, though low, was warm and pleasant on my face. We seemed to be walking on a gravel path. The soldiers kept a tight grip on my arms but said nothing. My mind was in a whirl and I couldn't think straight.

"When we were in the Chinese garrison before the Japs captured us, Hallmark, Meder and I had talked about the possibility of execution. We had told each other the Japs would surely kill us, but we really didn't believe it. Now it began to dawn on me that the Japs were perfectly capable of doing it and that they could easily get away with it. It's awful hard to understand that you are about to die, especially when you are not conscious of having done anything wrong. I didn't feel any fear then, just a numbness in my body and an empty feeling in my stomach.

"As we marched along I became aware that several men were marching behind me. I could hear the cadence of their steps and I knew they were soldiers. This is the firing squad, I thought, and my heart seemed to turn over and stop. My throat felt dry. I wanted to say something—ask a question, but I knew the soldiers wouldn't understand me and probably wouldn't answer if they did. We had marched about a thousand feet when I heard a guttural command and the men behind me halted.

I heard their rifle butts hit the gravel path. I was marched along a few feet farther and then brought to a halt.

"They turned me so that my back was squarely to the squad behind me. The blindfold was still on and I couldn't see what was in front of me. The sweat was pouring down my face and neck now. I wanted desperately to wipe my face but my hands were handcuffed and tied behind me. I heard another guttural command and I thought I could hear the slight noise of rifles being raised in position. I sensed that the guards were near me but I was not being held. The thought of trying to run came to my head but it was obviously a futile idea. My legs were still weak from the bamboo knee-spreading treatment, I couldn't get the blindfold off, I couldn't see which way to go and I was certain to be shot the moment I made a break. I almost collapsed. My whole life flashed in front of my mind's eye. I remembered how Dad and I used to go hunting and fishing back in Utah when I was a boy and the many things he taught me about wood lore and how we'd done so many things together, and how my mother would bake on Saturdays and how I would come home from a dance or a party and eat half her pies or cakes. I realized suddenly then that my folks would never know what had become of me and that thought was agonizing. Somehow I guess a man feels a little better if he is certain that those he loves know what happens to him.

"I began to feel real weak and nauseated. I thought my heart was actually going to stop. It would pound and jump and there seemed to be long pauses between the beats. Then I heard another command and this was followed by the sound of marching feet. A second later I heard the voice of the interpreter. He was laughing.

"'Well, well, well,' he said. 'We are the Knights of Bushido, of the Order of the Rising Sun. We do not execute men at sunset—only at sunrise. It's now sunset so your execution will take place in the morning. We will shoot you then unless you decide to talk in the meantime.'

"I drew a long breath and my heart began to slow down. Rage took the place of the fear I felt. Had it not been for the blindfold and the handcuffs, I would have taken a chance on slugging the interpreter then. I had been at the point of breaking, I suppose, but I felt real strength now, and I said to myself, 'If you boys don't shoot me now, you won't shoot me in the morning. In the meantime, if Nielsen gets a chance to get out of here, he's taking it.'

"The two guards marched me back to my cell and removed the blindfold. They brought me some ham sandwiches, a couple of vegetable sandwiches and a cup of coffee. The food tasted good. I worried a little about it being doped but I ate it anyway. I didn't know what was happening to Hallmark or Meder during the hours I was being questioned, but after I finished eating I heard Hallmark's voice down the corridor. They were putting him in his cell then. Those fellows received the same treatment I did and although I didn't know it at the moment, the Japs were getting us set up for the worst ordeal of all.

"About an hour later, three guards entered my cell. They were husky fellows and completely impassive like those in the torture room. They examined the handcuffs on my wrists and the chain between them, then they pushed me over to a wall of the cell and raised my arms above my head. There was a stout wooden peg in the wall that I hadn't noticed before and they boosted me up and hung me on the peg by the chain of the handcuffs. When they let me go my toes just barely touched the floor but not enough so that I could use any pressure to ease the strain on my arms.

"The guards didn't say a word. They looked at me a moment and then turned and left the cell, locking the door. Panic really seized me. I didn't think I could stand that pain for very long. There wasn't a thing to do and if I struggled I merely hurt myself more. In a few minutes the pain in my wrists was so intense that I was almost sick to my stomach, and then stabs of pain began to shoot in my chest and shoulders and my left arm that had been wounded in the airplane crash looked like it was getting blood poisoning in it, it was all swollen up and it really caused me more pain than anything else. I think I shouted several times but that didn't do any good either. I don't know how long I hung there before I passed out, but I know I was unconscious most of the night.

"They took me down about 6 o'clock the next morning. I couldn't stand at first but my legs recovered very fast; however, I had no use of my arms and I thought they would drop off when I slowly lowered them. They merely hung down and I couldn't move them. I felt pretty hopeless that morning, all done in. I was dirty and tired and I wondered if anything was worth this kind of treatment."

The guards put the blindfold back on Nielsen and led him to an anteroom where the blindfold was removed. Hallmark and Meder were there, disheveled, bruised and grim. All three men had grown beards on the *Hornet* but had kept them trimmed and clean. Now they looked like tramps. Although they couldn't talk they each gave the "thumbs up sign" which made them all feel better.

After a breakfast of sandwiches and coffee, they were blindfolded and led aboard a transport for the flight to Tokyo. They all were apprehensive and figured the tortures they would now experience would make the Shanghai treatment mild by comparison. Actually, a more subtle form of torture awaited them—endless days and nights of solitary confinement relieved only by the cruel interrogations, the pitifully inadequate meals and the yelling of the guards each time a prisoner was not found in a sitting position.

5
· · · · ·
"BLOW IT OUT YOUR
BARRACKS BAG, BUSTER!"

*B*ILL FARROW AND HIS CREW did not know that Dean Hallmark, Bob Meder and
Chase Nielsen had arrived in Tokyo. Stupefied and bewildered from the constant
beatings, exhausted from the questionings and weak from the systematic starvation
diet, they were not aware of much outside their own personal misery. However, the
five had now become eight and one by one each found out who the others were.

The fact that there were now eight Americans to interrogate caused the Japanese
to redouble their efforts to learn more about the Doolittle-led raid. Several new
"characters" were brought into the questioning sessions. One was named Ohara and
particularly stood out in the memories of the prisoners. He wore fancy shoes, the
plus-fours made famous during the Bobby Jones golf era and loud checked socks.
His task, like the half dozen other interpreters, was to elicit information one way
or another. Their usual method, since they could speak the American idiom, although
with a British accent, was to talk disarmingly about things they were familiar with
and then suddenly launch into probing questions with little or no transition. All
had been educated in the United States so many questions about geography could
be answered truthfully with the full knowledge that the interrogator already knew
the correct answer.

Bob Hite's description of the interrogation sessions and his reaction to them was
typical of all:

"After many hours of questioning and the beatings that always went with them,
I finally decided to agree with everything they said or wanted me to say. If they

volunteered some clue as to what answer they wanted me to give, I would give it—
no matter how fantastic it would be. When they asked me a direct question, I would
ask a question right back to see what kind of answer they expected and then give
it to them. They literally put words in my mouth.

"From the continual hammering away at questions about the *Hornet*, all of us felt
sure that they just couldn't believe that our B-25's could have taken off from a carrier.
This confusion was further compounded by the fact that we all insisted we had taken
off from the Aleutians. Nevertheless, the questions about the *Hornet* went on.

"A group of 'experts' on American history, politics, and geography was paraded
before us. While they may have been knowledgeable, they certainly had distorted
views of our heritage, culture, and economic growth but the greater the distortion,
the more we agreed to it.

"They brought in photographs of American aircraft carriers but none of the
Hornet. I guess it was so new that their spies hadn't yet been able to get photos of
it back to Japan. But they had an outline drawing of the *Hornet* and asked me to
tell them the dimensions, location of gun emplacements and crew arrangements below
deck. I made up all sorts of cockeyed stories from my imagination. Much to my surprise, they came back one day with a detailed engineering drawing based on all the
bum steers I had given them. It was a beaut! Any similarity between their drawing
and the real *Hornet* was a pure coincidence. What they didn't know was that since
my trip on the *Hornet* was the first time I had ever been on a ship of any kind, I
couldn't have helped them if I had really wanted to. If they ever built a carrier of
the dimensions and with the size guns that I gave them, the thing would never have
gotten out of drydock because it would have been so top heavy."

When the Kempei Tai finally began to realize that they were not getting verifiable
answers, they must have decided the prisoners needed rest. After four weeks of round-
the-clock interrogations, the prisoners were allowed to sleep at night but the dull
drone of daytime questioning continued. During the first week of June, the prisoners
were doubled up and their morale soared but they were extremely suspicious. Nielsen
and Farrow were put together in Cell #2, Hallmark and Meder in #3, Spatz and
DeShazer in #4. George Barr was put in Cell #1 with Bob Hite but for the first day
they didn't talk to each other. They checked every inch of the cell they could reach
searching for listening devices, while the guards outside watched. They found nothing
and when the guards relaxed their vigil, exchanged their first words with each other.
The guards quickly returned and began shouting, "Do not talk!"—obviously one
of several English phrases they had been ordered to memorize. But being together
was enough. Barr and Hite conversed in whispers and compared notes on their treatment and what they had told their captors.

The single most important thought in the minds of all the prisoners was whether or not they were going to be shot. They knew they were prize prisoners and they realized more than ever what a psychological blow the raid on their homeland was to the Japanese. They had "lost face" and that, to an Oriental, was a fate worse than death. If they weren't executed, each man figured that his chances of surviving Japanese prison under the conditions they had already experienced were slim. And because of their special status, they knew escape was impossible. Their Occidental features, beards, height and hair coloring would be difficult, if not impossible, to disguise in a part of the world where a Caucasian was a rare sight.

To add to their individual and collective miseries, all eight of the men had dysentery. Their diet had been reduced to six slices of bread and three cups of tea per day. They had not had a bath, shave or change of clothes since their capture and their beards and hair were now long and matted. The odor of their own bodies, the stench from the *benjo*, a hole in the floor serving as a toilet, and the humid atmosphere of the airless, lightless cells became overpowering. The only relief from this form of torture was the hours of questioning.

During the first part of June, each of the eight men was led from his cell to an interrogation room as usual. This time, however, there was a difference. Instead of questions, they were each seated at a table and handed a pen. The interpreter pushed a sheaf of papers forward, all written in Japanese, and told them to sign their names. As usual, guards lurked menacingly around the room. To a man they all asked the same question: "What is it?" They were given the same answer: "A confession." They were told simply that if they did not sign they would be shot at sunrise.

There is something about the word "confession" that is repugnant to most Americans and these eight airmen were no exception. They all balked and were promptly rewarded with slaps and kicks by the guards. By this time, however, nothing seemed to matter much. The papers before them, full of Japanese characters, had no meaning. None of them knew what the "confessions" said and none really cared any more.

It was not known until after the war that the Japanese had made up a question-and-answer interrogation based on the hours of grilling they had conducted. According to 7330 Noboro Unit Military Police Report No. 352, dated May 22, 1942, the eight captives had fully confessed their war crimes and admitted that they had bombed and strafed schools and hospitals instead of military targets. The falsification of the "confessions" is obvious as evidenced by the odd, stilted sentence structure and the fact that none of the men could speak, read or write the Japanese language. Following are excerpts from the Kempei Tai report which shows the strange colloquialism attributed to the prisoners and proves beyond a doubt that their fate was already sealed:

Q. Did you do any strafing while getting away from Nagoya?

Hite: Heretofore, I haven't revealed any information on this point, but the truth is that about five to six minutes after leaving the city we saw in the distance what looked like an elementary school with many children at play. The pilot steadily dropped altitude and ordered the gunmen to their stations. When the plane was at an oblique angle, the skipper gave firing orders, and bursts of machine gun fire sprayed the ground.

Q. While heading out to sea from Nagoya, didn't you strafe children of an elementary school?

Farrow: There is truly no excuse for this. I have made no mention of this before, but after leaving Nagoya, I do not quite remember the place—there was a place which looked like a school, with many people there. As parting shot, with a feeling of "damn these Japs," I made a power dive and carried out some strafing. There was absolutely no defensive fire from below.

Q. What are you thinking of after killing and wounding so many innocent people?

Hallmark: Since it was our intention to bomb Tokyo and escape to China quickly, we also dropped bombs over objectives other than those targets specified, and made a hasty escape. Therefore, we also bombed residential homes, killing, and wounding many people.

Q. After the bombing of Nagoya, did you not actually carry out strafing?

Spatz: It was an extremely inexcusable deed. Shortly after leaving Nagoya, while flying southward along the coast, the pilot immediately upon perceiving a school, steadily reduced altitude and ordered us to our stations. I aimed at the children in the school yard and fired only one burst before we headed out to sea. My feelings at that time were "damn these Japs" and I wanted to give them a burst of fire. Now I clearly see that this was truly unpardonable and in all decency should not have been committed.

Q. Even if you were instructed by the pilot to drop the bomb properly, didn't you as the bombardier, think that in the name of humanity you shouldn't have bombed innocent civilians?

DeShazer: With our technique and methods used in that air attack such things, even if we thought about them, would have been impossible.

Q. State the conditions at the time of the bombing.

Nielsen: At that time I was mainly observing the situation outside from the windows. At an altitude of 1,500 meters, as soon as we crossed the Noka River in the northeast part of Tokyo, the pilot frantically ordered the bombing. In general the main objective was the factories but with such a bombing method, I believe we missed it completely.

Q. You not only bombed the factories, but you also bombed homes of innocent civilians and killed many people. What are your reactions in that respect?

Meder: It is natural that dropping bombs on a crowded place like Tokyo will cause damage in the vicinity of the target. All the more so with our technique of dropping bombs while making a hit-and-run attack, so I believe it was strictly unavoidable. Moreover, Colonel Doolittle never did order us to avoid such bombings and neither were we particularly worried about the possible damage.

Q. Did you not strafe an elementary school while headed out to sea after the Nagoya raid?

Barr: I am quite sure that was done. Only when the pilot steadily dropped altitude and the strafing was executed was I aware of it.

From the moment the papers were signed the interrogations ceased. One week later, on June 15th, the eight Americans were given their shoes and socks, handcuffed and legcuffed in pairs and taken into the prison courtyard where they were photographed. They were then led to four cars—a Chevrolet and three Fords—and taken to a railroad station. Their arms and legs ached because the cuffs were too small but the guards were not concerned as they led them aboard a train crowded with hundreds of Japanese civilians who stared at them stoically. They were given some fruit and a small lunch box containing rice, daikon, sakana and shredded cabbage. It was the first decent meal they had had in weeks and they ate ravenously.

The train began a journey that lasted two days. Each pair of prisoners was crowded into a seat with a guard sitting alongside them on the aisle. People from adjacent cars looked through tile doors at each end of the car and the sergeant of the guard warned them away. When his admonishments went unheeded, he finally plastered newspaper over the glass.

It was a miserable two days as the train lurched and tumbled through the countryside. They left the train and took a ferry to the island of Kyushu for another day of train riding to Nagasaki. There they were all herded into a hot, stinking cell overnight and loaded aboard a small freighter the next morning for the two-day trip to Shanghai. They were well-treated and well-fed during this part of their journey and were allowed to converse freely. While they were happy being together, they expressed mutual doubts about their future—not only their own but the United States' as well. Japan had been fighting for over a decade and had five million men under arms. The United States had only about a million men in uniform when they had left home and was not geared to a war economy. How long would the war last? Could the United States win it? How long could the eight of them hold out? If the war lasted more than five years, the consensus was that they couldn't last that long if the conditions in the prison they were going to were similar to those they had experienced so far. And then there was always the possibility that they would still be executed as their captors had threatened so many times. As they steamed along each man hoped that an American submarine would fire a torpedo into the ship and give them a chance, maybe a final chance, to escape.

The capture of the eight Doolittle fliers had caused quite a stir in Japanese officialdom. One faction of the Japanese Army felt the invasion of their homeland by American planes was a personal affront. They had bragged to one another and the civilian populace that Japan would never be invaded. Now American planes had not only invaded their skies, but had bombed their war industries and precious oil supplies. Worse than that, the Americans had placed the Emperor and his family in grave personal danger. To their way of thinking, this "war crime" was so dastardly that there was only one punishment—death.

General Sugiyama, Chief of the General Staff, was particularly enraged and immediately referred to the attack as "indiscriminate bombing." He had directed the Japanese Army commanders in occupied China to leave no stone unturned to apprehend any members. When the eight luckless men were reported captured he had wired that "all the investigations and punishments in regard to the raids will be conducted by our military staff headquarters in Tokyo."

The basic question to be decided was whether the captured airmen should be tried as "prisoners of war" or "war criminals." If declared the former, they could not suffer the death penalty for an act of war and were to be accorded the rights of prisoners of war under the Geneva Convention. If the latter, their fate would be whatever a Japanese court wanted it to be, with death the most likely.

Sugiyama insisted these men were war criminals and should be executed without delay. However, General Hideki Tojo, then Premier, argued for lighter sentences. Since it appeared that Sugiyama was going to come off second best, confessions by the officers themselves might allow him to get his way. It can only be assumed that the Kempei Tai had been ordered to get the confessions by making the captives sign the pages of meaningless Japanese characters. With such evidence, Sugiyama was confident that he would win his argument. He reasoned that killing civilians was an act of murder, not an act of war. The Americans had admitted their crimes. Therefore they should be executed as war criminals.

It will probably never be known exactly what argument went on in Tokyo concerning the fate of these men. But while the eight Americans were returning to China, the "confessions" were being studied at the highest level of the Japanese military system. Legal officers were asked their opinions concerning what rules of international law applied to this case which would make the death penalty permissible and justifiable.

They found that there were no laws specifically covering raids by enemy airmen. Therefore a law would have to be made up and applied after the fact.

The ship containing the eight Doolittle fliers docked in the busy Shanghai harbor on June 19th. There were many ships in the harbor, including some half-submerged English freighters which had been caught when the war began. After the other passengers disembarked, the prisoners were taken ashore and locked in a warehouse until a truck came to take them to the Bridge House, a former English hotel that had been taken over by the Japanese and made into a military headquarters and jail. There they were thrust into a cell about 10′×15′ containing three Chinese women, one Japanese man, several young Chinese boys and a Russian by the name of Alexander Hindrava, who spoke English, Chinese, and Japanese.

The stench and the heat of the dark, crowded cell was overpowering as the eight men were pushed inside. The *benjo* in one corner was overflowing and this combined with the body odors of the other occupants and their own, caused them to retch. Now that there were about thirty people crowded into the cell there was no place to lie down. One elderly Chinese man, nearly dead from dysentery, lay immobile on the floor. The only thing to do was take turns sitting down.

The next three days were nightmarish as the six officers and two enlisted men assessed their situation. Still bruised from the tortures in Tokyo and weakened by the inadequate diet, they had only one consolation. They were all together and could talk to one another freely for the first time—that is, when the guards were not listening. These men were special prisoners, the first American military airmen incarcerated in Shanghai. They had bombed Tokyo. Every guard in the headquarters detachment wanted to see them. At all hours of the day and night, Japanese faces peered in the small barred peephole. If the Americans were talking or whispering the guards would yell and beat on the door but never dared to unlock it. When the fliers discovered this, they continued to talk in defiance.

Actually, the enforced togetherness was good for their morale. The three men of Dean Hallmark's crew told the story of their crash landing at sea, the loss of the two enlisted crewmen, and the subsequent capture of the three officers. Bill Farrow and his men described their bailout and attempts to evade capture. All of them discussed the tortures they had received and the lies they had told the gullible Japanese interrogators.

But the mere privilege of free talk was not enough and morale began to sag noticeably after the first day. The condition of the other prisoners bothered the relatively healthy Americans. All of them were in rags and their bodies were covered with huge scabs and open sores. They seemed too weak even to talk to each other. Hindrava, the Russian, was reluctant to give any information about the reasons for their imprisonment and was unable to explain why he had been sentenced and thrust into this hell hole.

Food and water soon became the major concern for the Americans. Meals, if they could be called that, were "served" three times a day. The menu consisted solely of yellowed watery rice and weak tea. The rice was obviously taken from the scrapings left after meals had been prepared for the prison staff. Served in chipped enamel pans, the yellow grains were mixed with pebbles, worms, maggots and dirt. To a man, the Americans' reactions were identical. They took one look at the wriggling, crawling things and handed their bowls to their Oriental cellmates who promptly scooped them clean and grinned in silent gratitude.

The tea, of dubious origin, was not given away. The extreme heat of the cell had so dehydrated them all that they would have drunk anything that even resembled a liquid. Although the taste was bitter, it quenched their thirst, but it was scarcely life-sustaining.

It was Chase Nielsen who first decided that their survival depended on their managing somehow to eat the unappetizing food thrust at them through the slot in the door. "It may not be what we eat at home," he told his buddies, "but it's got some food value and we'll die if we don't eat anything. Every grain of that lousy rice has something our bodies need and even the worms might have a vitamin or two. I don't know about you guys but I intend to stay alive and someday tell the world what the Japs have done to us here!"

Nielsen's attitude was contagious and one by one the other seven men managed to down the watery rice, dirt, maggots, and all. The worms became delicacies because, as Bob Hite recalled, "at least they had a little fat on them."

After three days in the filth and stench of the crowded cell, where the monotony of the hours was broken only by the shouting of the guards when they caught the prisoners talking or the clatter of the pans as they shoved them through the door slot, the civilian prisoners were taken out of the cell and led away. For the first time since their capture, the eight Americans were now alone and could stretch their legs out and lie down. There was a small consolation in this because it meant that they could discuss their plight without fear that one of their cell mates was a spy. Each time they talked out loud, however, the guards would bang on the door and shout in Japanese, "Kurah!" (hey!). Although they were obviously instructed to keep all prisoners quiet, none of them ever opened the door to enforce the rule. As a result, Bob Hite, quick-tempered Texan who was chafing bitterly about their treatment, shouted back at the guards in defiance one day. The two guards outside quickly multiplied to a half dozen. There was more shouting and rattling of the cell door but nothing else.

Confident now that they had bluffed the guards, they made no effort to keep quiet. And although the guards ranted and raved outside, the Americans only laughed and continued their discussions. It helped their morale considerably and enabled them all to know each other better. To while away the time, each man told of his life in great detail. George Barr, orphaned at an early age when his father was lost while fishing off Long Island, told of living in a home for boys until he went to college with the help of his unofficial foster parents, Mr. and Mrs. Charles A. Towns. The tall, raw-boned navigator modestly told of his athletic successes at Northland College in Ashland, Wisconsin, and his hopes to be a high school teacher and coach someday.

Jacob DeShazer, son of an Oregon lay minister and farmer, recalled his carefree days hunting and fishing with his father. He admitted that he had never taken school seriously and had joined the Air Force for want of something better to do. His proudest accomplishments were completing the airplane mechanic and bombardier schools. Quiet and reserved, it took much prying to get Jake to talk about himself.

Bill Farrow, a tall, lanky South Carolinian, was an easy-going pilot who was well liked by all who knew him. He was respected for his philosophical views of life and his ability to mediate differences of opinion. He had attended the University of South Carolina for two years and had joined the Air Force as a Flying Cadet and won his wings at Kelly Field, Texas, in July, 1941. He talked of his fiancee longingly and told of his plans to marry her when the war was over. He recalled the delicious meals his widowed mother, Mrs. Jessie Farrow, used to cook and the mere mention of food would stimulate the others to describe their favorite meal that they now missed so much.

Farrow's co-pilot, Bob Hite, called Earth, Texas, his home town and was proud of the fact that he had been reared in ranch country. He loved the outdoors and talked longingly of the great plains where there were "no fences and the people never locked their doors." An aggressive individual, Hite was a man of quick decisions and an occasionally volatile temper to whom imprisonment was a personal insult and an effrontery to his basic nature. His bitterness at being cooped up sometimes overwhelmed him and caused him to be argumentative at times with his buddies. Highly intelligent, he had completed three years at Texas State College before entering pilot training but loved the Air Force and planned to make it a career.

The other Texan in the group was Dean Hallmark, a husky, black-haired ruddy-faced individual who was older than the others. Nicknamed "Jungle Jim," he walked with a swagger that fitted his personality. He talked freely of his boyhood and his college days spent at junior college in Paris, Texas, and Alabama Polytechnic Institute. He, too, recalled his mother's home cooking, with lip-smacking gusto with special mention of her biscuits and gravy, bacon and eggs and stewed apricots—his favorite breakfast. His mention of syrup pies and vinegar cobblers was strange to most of the others but Hite assured them they hadn't tasted true Texas cooking yet and could be excused for their ignorance of such delicacies.

Hallmark, like the others, liked the life of an Air Force flier and planned to stay in the service after the war. He had been undecided about the future while attending college and admitted he had not found his niche in life and had been caught in the contagion of joining the service when he passed the stiff pilot physical exam and began his primary training. "My only regret is that I didn't join sooner," he told his fellow prisoners. "If I had, I would probably be a captain by now. Then I'd be getting more pity for being in this miserable hole than the rest of you guys."

Bob Meder, Hallmark's co-pilot, was almost a direct opposite in personality. Quiet and reserved, the tall, well-built Ohioan had graduated from college. He had been a track man and popular with his school mates. Memories of his childhood days in northern Ohio came easily and he recalled many of the good times he had had with his gang. His reminiscences always sparked similar stories from the others and helped make the hours go by more easily.

Another of the Tokyo Raid prisoners who loved the outdoor life was Chase Nielsen, who had the dark complexion and hair of an American Indian, but was actually of Swedish descent. Born and reared in Utah, he had studied civil engineering at Utah State University before joining the service in August 1939. He had enlisted as a Flying Cadet, had gone on to navigation school and was commissioned in June, 1941. He planned to remain in the service when the war was over but he fully intended to return eventually to Utah and "settle down forever where the sky is blue, the mountains are tall and a man's only limitation is his own imagination."

A man who likes to talk and can express himself admirably, Nielsen possessed one characteristic that was to contribute to his survival and eventual release. He had the will to live, born not of mere self-preservation, but of a deep-seated hatred for his captors and the fact that he and his fellows had been reduced to an animal existence when they should have been treated as war prisoners instead of war criminals. In reminiscing about the past, he vowed that the Japanese responsible for their condition would be made to pay someday. The bitterness at being confined colored his memories of the carefree days of his youth and made him seethe with anger and frustration.

The only other enlisted man in the group besides Jake DeShazer was Sergeant Harold A. Spatz, 22-year-old Kansan who had been top turret gunner on Farrow's plane. He had clear blue eyes, medium build, and the same quiet manner as DeShazer. One of the youngest men on the raid, he had graduated from high school in Lebo, Kansas, in 1939 and entered the army at Ft. Riley a few months later. He had transferred to the Army Air Forces and completed mechanic's training in March, 1941. His father was a farmer, his mother had died when he was quite young, and life for him during the depression years had not been easy. But he was not at all bitter about his youth. He had worked hard but he had played hard. However, he liked service life and did not plan to return to the rural life he had known.

The open and free disclosures of each man's background was a good catharsis. It made them all realize that behind the exterior of each man there was a human being who had grown up with the same hopes, ambitions, desires and fears as the others. While they were from different parts of the country, they were Americans who were united in spirit and compassion. Whatever their fate, each now knew the others better and felt a bond which was enhanced by their common plight.

The ordeal in the Bridge House lasted seventy days. During that time they had not been out of the cell, still had not been able to wash, shave, or take off their clothes. Their bodies were covered with welts from the lice and bedbugs which infected the cell and nested in their clothes. Although it was hot, they would stuff their trousers in their socks and button their collars and cuffs to keep from being literally devoured by thousands of crawling insects that would come out at night. Days were spent picking them out of the seams of clothes and smashing them, whenever they could be seen.

The rats were far more a menace than the bugs, however. A pack of them lived under the cell floor and would emerge from the benjo at night. Their quarry was not the men but the grains of rice that had slipped into the cracks in the floor. As the men lay in a row, the rats would sniff and eat their way along a crack until they came to a body. They would nibble away at whatever was exposed until they were beaten off or found something better. After a few bouts with them in the dark, it was decided that every man would take turns staying awake an hour each night to keep the rodents away from their sleeping buddies.

The starvation diet soon began to tell on each man. Their faces grew gaunt behind the shaggy beards and belts were tightened notch after notch. Fortunately, the guards slackened their vigil and almost became friendly. Every once in a while, however, a new guard would come on duty and try to enforce the no-talking rule only to be laughed at and jeered by the Americans because they never came inside the cell. One of them must have reported the talking one day for as soon as the guard started yelling, Bob Hite shouted right back: "Blow it out your barracks bag, buster!"

The guard screamed some more and Hite smashed at the barred slot in the door with his fist. As he did, the door flew open and a Japanese officer rushed in and slashed at Hite with his scabbard, leaving a nasty scalp wound. It was all Hite's hair-trigger temper needed. He grabbed the scabbard and wrenched it away, leaving the unsheathed sword gleaming and ready to plunge into Hite's midriff.

There was a pause as the prisoners held their breath. To a man, they had the same thought. If he stabbed Hite, the rest of them were going to strangle him before the other guards could rush in. In one stride Farrow was beside Hite ready to share the next blow. Both slouching low like wrestlers, they waited for something to happen. Blood streamed down Hite's forehead. Sensing what the prisoners were thinking, the officer quickly backed out of the cell and slammed the door.

The encounter had been brief and unexpected. It seemed to accomplish nothing, yet from that point on, the guards were somehow more reasonable. Some became friendly and the friendliness developed into a windfall.

It was the constant thought of food that obsessed the prisoners more than anything. "We thought about it," Nielsen recalls, "we talked about it, we dreamed about it but we didn't eat it. We mentally planned the meals we would eat when we got out — big juicy steaks with plenty of pie and ice cream."

Strangely and without any notice, instead of the usual watery rice edition, a new fare was shoved through the hole in the cell door. It had been provided by the Shanghai Municipal Police, mostly Englishmen who were still allowed on duty in the international city to maintain law and order among the civilian populace. They had taken up a collection for food for every English or American prisoner held by the Japanese. For fourteen days, once a day, the eight prisoners had a good meal which included fresh corn, deviled eggs, meat, dessert and hot coffee or tea. They never were able to thank their benefactors or learn who was responsible, but their kindness was appreciated more than words could express. Just as it had begun without notice, the good food ceased. The guards gave no clues and morale sagged once more.

One day several weeks later, as the eight men sat around brooding, one of them wondered if the guards could be bribed with American money. Strangely, most of them had been allowed to keep their paper money although their change, wallets, watches and rings had been taken when they were first captured. It was worth a try.

It took three weeks to arrange it but one of the sergeants of the guard who understood a little English agreed to see if he could exchange the American dollars on the black market. The prisoners could only pray that he would come through and he did. They said they wanted meat, sweets, haircuts, a bath, clean shorts, socks, and shirts. Mysteriously, they got all they asked for although the food did not last long. The sweets were candy bars, which they saved to eat when rations got short again, only to find that they were moldy when the wrappers were removed. But the few dollars spent proved to be worth many times their value in improved morale. Bob Hite recalls what happened:

"I don't think any of us will ever forget the thrill of that first bath—the first in over 120 days. We were taken one at a time up to a fourth floor hotel room and allowed to stay as long as we wanted. As I remember I used a cake and a half of soap and I don't remember a kinder feeling than the soothing wet warmth of that tub. I changed the water two or three times and still when I got out there was a thick scum on the top and the tub was black with lice.

"They clipped our beards that day, too, and shaved our heads. We got a change of clothes and felt like new men. That afternoon, we got the thing we had sought— a real feed. There was steak, fresh vegetables, strawberry jam and French bread. The sheer joy of spreading that strawberry jam on that bread will remain with me always."

A few hours after the feast, their last in captivity, Dean Hallmark complained of stomach pains. His temperature soared and he developed an unmanageable case of dysentery. Several times during the night he was overcome with vomiting and fell head long into the *benjo*. The others took turns helping him back and forth to the *benjo*. By morning, he was so weak he couldn't get up. His joints ached and he fainted frequently. There were no blankets in the cell so the rest of the men made a pallet for him out of their jackets. They took turns talking to him and when he would pass out, they would try to bring him to. By the end of the third day, Hallmark looked like a skeleton. He had weighed 200 pounds when he had been captured. He now looked as if he weighed about 140.

It was August 28th by now, a day they would remember. Without warning they were loaded aboard a truck, including Hallmark whom Farrow and Hite carried on a stretcher, and were taken to the Kiangwan military prison, also known as the Ward Road jail. Unknown to them, they were to be the first Americans tried under a law that had just been enacted to take care of their "crime." Not only the verdict but the sentence had already been prescribed.

6
· · · · ·
TRIAL AND CONSEQUENCES

*T*HE "CONFESSIONS" TAKEN from the eight Doolittle fliers on May 22nd had been studied in the Japanese Ministry of War for two months before a decision was reached. The legal experts had not been able to find precedents for accusing the American airmen as war criminals. Therefore, the accusation could only be made by establishing a law and then applying it *ex post facto* to the Doolittle raiders.

On July 28, 1942, Heitaro Kimura, Vice-Minister of War, dispatched Military Secret Order No. 2190 to Army headquarters in Tokyo directing that "An enemy warplane crew who did not violate wartime international law, shall be treated as prisoners of war, and one who acted against the said law shall be punished as a wartime capital criminal." Upon receipt of this directive, Seibu Tanabe, Assistant Chief of Staff of the Grand Imperial Headquarters, sent the order to General Sunao Ushiromiya, Chief of Staff of the Expeditionary Army in China. He appended a memo (Staff Document No. 383-1) which was further proof that the fate of the Americans had already been decided:

> In regard to Military Secret Order No. 2190 concerning the disposition of the captured enemy airmen, request that action be deferred (probably until the middle of August) pending proclamation of the military law and its official announcement, *and the scheduling of the date of execution of the American airmen.* (Italics furnished.)

While the Tokyo Raiders languished in the Bridge House, unaware that they had already been earmarked to die, the legal officers at Grand Imperial Headquarters finally agreed on the wording of what was to be known as the Enemy Airmen's Act. On August 13, 1942, General Shunroku Hata, Supreme Commander of Japanese Forces in China, allowed his chop to be affixed to Military Ordinance No. 4 so that it could be applied immediately to his theater of operations specifically for Doolittle's men:

Military Law Concerning the Punishment of Enemy Airmen

Art. I. This military law shall apply to all enemy airmen who raid the Japanese homeland, Manchukuo, and the Japanese zones of military operations, and who come within the areas under the jurisdiction of the China Expeditionary Force.

Art. II. Any individual who commits any or all of the following acts shall be subject to military punishment:

Sec. 1. The bombing, strafing, and otherwise attacking of civilians with the objective of cowing, intimidating, killing or maiming them.

Sec. 2. The bombing, strafing or otherwise attacking of private properties whatsoever, with the objectives of destroying or damaging same.

Sec. 3. The bombing, strafing or otherwise attacking of objectives, other than those of military nature, except in those cases where such an act is unavoidable.

Sec. 4. In addition to those acts covered in the preceding three sections, all other acts violating the provisions of International Law governing warfare.

This law shall also apply to those individuals who raid Japan proper, Manchukuo, and the Japanese zones of military operation with the intent of committing such acts, and who prior to accomplishing their objective come within the jurisdiction of the China Expeditionary Force.

Art. III. Military punishment shall be the death penalty, provided however, should the circumstances warrant, this sentence may be commuted to life imprisonment, or a term of imprisonment for not less than 10 years.

Art. IV. The death penalty shall be executed by a firing squad. Imprisonment shall be in confinement in a penitentiary for the term of sentence.

Art. V. Under extraordinary circumstances military punishment may be waived.

Art. VI. In regard to the imprisonment, in addition to the stipulation prescribed under this military law, the rules and regulations of penal law shall also apply. This military law shall be effective as of 13 August 1942.

This military law shall be applicable to all acts committed prior to the date of its approval.

The legal justification to hold a trial and satisfy the Japanese conscience for military justice in retaliation for the air raid on their homeland was now complete. Orders were passed to Shanghai to hold the trial on August 28th. Chase Nielsen describes what happened:

"It was a sunny, pleasant day as they handcuffed us and loaded us on the trucks. We asked the guards where we were going but got no answer. The guards were solemn. I felt sure that we were going to be executed and kept thinking of a way to escape, my heart sank as the truck passed through the gates of Kiangwan Military Prison and I saw them slam shut.

"We were pushed and shoved into a small courtroom and stood in a row before five Japanese officers sitting behind a long table on a raised platform. Dean Hallmark was carried in on the stretcher and laid on the floor. The flies buzzed all over him but he was too weak to brush them away. I'm sure he had no idea where he was or what was going on.

"It took no imagination to know that we were the principals in a military trial although we were not told so. The room was crowded with armed guards and officers all looking at us with their inscrutable faces devoid of emotion. The man in the center of the group of five was obviously the chief judge. A man about fifty years old, he was baldheaded and wore glasses down on the end of his nose. The other four men were younger and wore black wigs which made them look ridiculous.

"George Barr got so weak standing there that he keeled over and he was given a chair to sit on. The rest of us managed to stay on our feet—how, I'll never know. The room was swimming in front of me and I had a hard time keeping my balance.

"The judge began a long spiel in Japanese and we wondered what he was saying. When he finished he nodded to a Japanese standing at the side of the room who stepped forward and told us in English, to give a brief history of our lives from the time we were in high school. Each one of us, except Hallmark, mumbled our stories but we were so weak that we had to repeat many times. Nobody was writing anything down so I couldn't see that what we said mattered. The only thing I could figure was that it was all part of the ritual required in a Military Court Martial. The interpreter dutifully translated what we said to the judge who just stared at us. The other four sitting with him were obviously bored by the whole affair.

"I don't know what they expected from us, but most of us told the truth about ourselves until we got to our military service. We double-talked and lied but it didn't seem to make any difference. The judges were obviously disinterested and couldn't have cared less. None of us mentioned anything about the raid on Japan and the interpreter never asked us about it. Hallmark was not questioned.

"After the seven of us were finished, the judge read a statement which the interpreter said was the verdict and our sentences. Since the verdict seemed to be a foregone conclusion, I asked what our sentence was but he only smirked and said the judge had ordered that we not be told!"

The seven men were led to an adjoining building and placed in single cells. Hallmark was carried out on his stretcher and taken back to the Bridge House jail where he was placed in Cell No. 6 with twenty other prisoners of assorted nationalities. Alexander J. Sterelny, a Soviet National who had been imprisoned by the Japanese "for supporting my British colleagues with money" had been an accountant for Shanghai Dock Yards, Ltd. The 66-year-old Sterelny testified after the war as follows:

Q. Please state to the Commission what regulations the Japanese had with respect to how the prisoners in Cell No. 6 would conduct themselves in the cell.

A. Well, first of all, we were not allowed to speak to each other. We could not sit together.

Q. Were you permitted to walk around?

A. Yes.

Q. Did Lt. Hallmark walk around?

A. No, he never walked around, he couldn't.

Q. Were any of the prisoners permitted to take any exercise outside Cell No. 6?

A. No, not permitted.

Q. State to the Commission, if you remember, how much of the time Lt. Hallmark spent lying down.

A. All the time.

Q. Describe to the Commission what he looked like.

A. He was very thin and he had a beard as big as that (indicating by placing his right hand across the middle of his chest), black.

Q. Can you state to the Commission what was his approximate weight?

A. Well, I should judge him to be about 120 pounds.

Q. How tall was Hallmark?

A. I saw him straight up only once when he walked out of the cell, but he must be about five ten and a half, maybe five eleven.

Q. Did anyone help him out of his cell?

A. No, nobody, he walked himself. But he walked like a drunken man.

Q. During the time that you were in Cell No. 6 with Lt. Hallmark, did he have a change of clothing?

A. No, he did not.

Q. At any time was he washed or sponged off with water or anything else?

A. We had a bucket of water every morning for everybody—one bucket for the foreigners and one bucket for the Chinese. Well, the foreigners used that one bucket of water for all of us, then we had to wash our faces, our hands, our teeth, and so forth. As much as it lasted, it lasted. That was all.

Q. Can you state to the Commission anything with respect to the intestinal or bowel condition of Lt. Hallmark as you have observed it?

A. Well, it was mostly loose; he had a loose stomach.

At Kiangwan, the other seven prisoners were kept in solitary confinement for twenty days and then permitted to leave their cells individually for exercise a few minutes each day. The three meals per day were similar to and no better than those

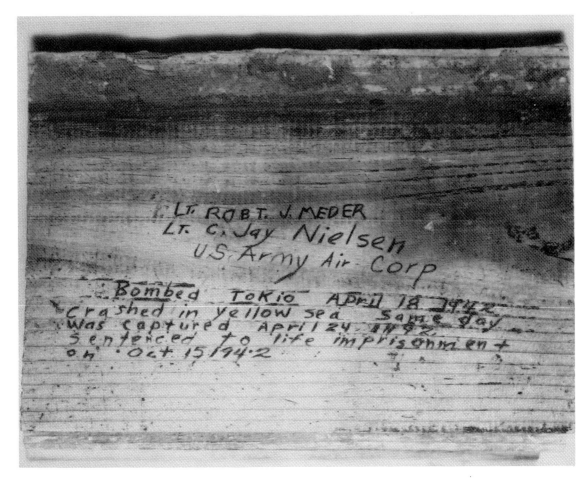

This photo shows a piece of flooring removed from the cell occupied by Lt. Chase J. Nielsen for use as evidence at the Japanese War Crimes Trials in 1946. Nielsen made the inscription with a nail on a section of the floor that the guards could not see. His purpose was "to leave some sort of record that other captured Americans might see and remember so that someone would know we had at least survived that long. If we died or were later executed, some record would be left behind as to where we had been and what happened." USAF Photo

at Bridge House: a glob of dirty rice and a watery soup. The monotonous diet and the deadly routine of inactivity in the six-by-nine-foot cells soon began to tell on the men. Worst of all was the nothingness of solitary confinement where they could see nothing but the four walls and the sky through a small window about seven feet from the floor. Nielsen described these days as "Get up at 6 A.M. Breakfast at 8. Exercise with a guard between 10:30 and 11. Lunch at 12. Supper at 5. Bed down at 9:30. The rest of the time we had nothing to do and nothing is the hardest thing in the world to do."

Three of Doolittle's Raiders were executed by a Japanese firing squad at a Chinese cemetery. The three persons shown here are posing in the same manner as Lts. Hallmark and Farrow and Sgt. Spatz when they were readied for execution. This photo, taken at Kiangwan Cemetery, Shanghai, China in December 1945, was used as evidence at the war crimes trials in 1946. The man on the left is Caesar dos Remedios who had also been a prisoner and secretly helped ease the misery of the Raiders. His testimony helped convict four of the Japanese guards responsible for cruelty toward the Raiders. USAF PHOTO

After the "trial" had been held, Lt. Col. Toyama Nakajo, the chief judge, signed the record of the trial which stated that the defendants "have been found guilty as charged, and are hereby sentenced to death." Under the heading of "reasons for the sentence," the record charged that the defendants, "motivated by their sporting instincts and sense of glory" had volunteered for the raid on Japan. Over their assigned targets, the defendants "suddenly exhibited cowardice when confronted with opposition in the air and on the ground, and with the intent of cowing, killing and wounding innocent civilians, and wreaking havoc on residences and other living quarters

An interior view of the cell block at Peiping (Peking) Prison, occupied by the surviving members of the two captured crews. Note the high windows in the cell wall and the slits in the heavy doors through which food was passed to the prisoners. PHOTO COURTESY COL. J. J. JACKSON

of no military significance whatsoever, together with other planes did carry on indiscriminate bombing and strafing, thereby causing the death and injury of about ten civilians, and the destruction of numerous residences." The final irony of the record is the statement that "the foregoing facts are based on the (1) depositions made by the eight defendants at the trial, and (2) the copy of the acknowledgement made by the Shanghai Military Police unit in response to the request of the Military Police Headquarters for full information as to the extent of damages and injuries sustained in said affair."

On October 10th, the Chief of the Imperial General Staff sent a telegram to the Commanding General of the China Expeditionary Force:

Exterior view of prison compound at Kiangwan Prison, Shanghai showing washing facilities to the left and prison block to right. Open area in foreground is part of exercise ground. USAF PHOTO

THE VERDICT BY THE MILITARY TRIBUNAL CONCERNING THE PUNISHMENT OF THE AMERICAN AIRMEN WHO RAIDED THE JAPANESE HOMELAND IS CONSIDERED TO BE FAIR AND JUST.

HOWEVER, UPON REVIEW WE BELIEVE THAT WITH THE EXCEPTION OF BOTH PILOTS AND THE GUNNER, SPATZ, THE DEATH SENTENCE SHOULD BE COMMUTED. IT IS RECOMMENDED THAT THE DEATH SENTENCES OF THESE MEN BE COMMUTED TO LIFE IMPRISONMENT.

A separate wire from General Sugiyama to General Hata was sent shortly thereafter and directed that the execution of Hallmark, Farrow, and Spatz was to take place on October 15th. It further stipulated that the five whose sentences were commuted

Door leading into George Barr's cell at Peiping, China. Guards watched prisoners through slit in door. Prisoners were required to sit on small stools and face the wall; they were beaten for non-compliance. USAF Photo

This photo was taken of inscription left on a floor board in Lt. Robert J. Meder's cell at Kiangwan Prison in Shanghai. The board was located by American investigators and used as evidence to prove that the Doolittle Raiders had occupied the prison. Meder died in prison of malnutrition and beri-beri. The inscription was found during the war crimes trials at Shanghai in 1946. PHOTO COURTESY CHASE J. NIELSEN

to life imprisonment "are adjudged as war criminals and as such should receive no consideration as prisoners of war." The final portion of the message ordered that "in no case will they be repatriated as prisoners of war in the event of an exchange of prisoners."

General Hata then had his staff write General Order No. 538 on October 14th, announcing confirmation of the original sentence of death for the three and mitigation of the sentence to life imprisonment for Meder, Nielsen, Hite, Barr, and DeShazer. The order further directed the prison warden that "in making this announcement to the convicted men, special mention must be made of the Emperor's leniency."

In all of the records concerning the Doolittle fliers, no reasons were ever given why Hallmark, Farrow and Spatz had been singled out for execution. It can only be surmised that inferences were drawn from the fake confessions that led members of the Imperial General Staff to rationalize that both pilots were guilty of the alleged war crimes because they guided the planes to their targets. Spatz had admitted that his duty had been as a gunner and therefore the most logical one to have done any strafing. DeShazer, the only other enlisted crew survivor, had been a bombardier but his faked statement made no mention that he had access to or had fired a machine gun from his position in the nose of the plane. Taken at face value at the highest level of the Japanese Government, the faked statements were the only evidence available upon which to base a decision to make three of the eight men pay the supreme penalty.

Now that the orders had been issued, they had only to be carried out in the best Japanese tradition. On the afternoon of October 14th, Hallmark was brought to Kiangwan and placed in a cell. One by one, he, Farrow and Spatz were taken to an adjoining storeroom and informed that they had been sentenced to death and would be executed the next day. They were given sheets of paper and pencils and then introduced to Caesar Luis dos Remedios, a Portuguese-Japanese who had been sentenced to seven years imprisonment for spying. Remedios was told to explain that each man could write letters to his friends and relatives. In later testimony, Remedios described what happened:

> On 14 October 1942 I was instructed by Sergeant Sotojiro Tatsuta (later Captain) to have Lt. Farrow, Lt. Hallmark, and Sgt. Spatz sign their names on two blank sheets of white paper. One page was signed by each of them in the middle of the sheet, and the other page was signed by each at the bottom. They asked me why they were made to sign these papers. Tatsuta told me that they were signing these as a receipt for their belongings and that he would fill the rest in Japanese later on.
>
> Later Tatsuta gave each two sheets of paper, one on which to write a letter to their family, which he said he would send through the Red Cross; and the other sheet was to be used to describe the treatment they received by the Japanese while they were confined. At that time I didn't know what the Japanese were going to do to these three airmen. The fliers asked me what they should write. My opinion was to give a little 'top hat' for the Japanese, so that they would be given good treatment later on. I didn't read the letters, but gave them to Sgt. Tatsuta early the next morning.

The shock of the announcement to these three emaciated airmen can only be imagined. Each wrote poignant farewell messages to their loved ones which show the mental agony they were going through. Farrow wrote to his mother in Darlington, S.C. telling her "Don't let this get you down. Remember God will make everything right and that I will see you all again in the hereafter. My faith in God is complete so I am not afraid."

To his good friend Ivan Ferguson, a squadron mate when stationed at Pendleton, Oregon, he wrote:

". . . Remember those days at Kelly Field with Rowe, R. B. Brown and the rest? . . . And do you remember Spokane and Glacier Park, and what we said about a place full of so much that is good and beautiful—what it's worth to us? And Crater Lake, Oregon Caves, the giant Sequoias, the Golden Gate—how splendid they were? And the thrill of flying that we experienced together, too—it was the most wonderful part of my career."

Farrow asked Ferguson to write to his mother saying "she will need your sympathy." He then wrote to his aunt, Miss Margaret Stem, also of Darlington, telling her that she had always been an inspiration to him and ended by saying "goodbye to all of you—I'm sorry it had to happen this way."

Hardest letter of all to write must have been the one addressed to his fiancee, then living in Columbia, S.C. He wrote:

"You are to me the only girl that would have meant the completion of my life. . . . Comfort Mom because she will need you . . . and find yourself the good man you deserve."

Harold Spatz wrote a letter to his widower father, Robert A. Spatz of Lebo, Kansas, saying that he had nothing to leave him but his clothes. Then he added: "I want you to know I died fighting for my country like a soldier." To please the Japanese he wrote a second note that "we go out every morning to wash and brush our teeth and we get out to exercise in the sunshine about every day." He added that "we are getting good food here" and closed with the observation that "it's sure nice of them to let us write letters home." Spatz also wrote one-sentence notes to his girl friend and brother, Robert, Jr. To his sister, Reba, he said, "I will say my last goodbye to you and may you live a happy life and God bless you."

Hallmark's bitterness at the verdict showed through in his farewell letter to his mother, father and sister in Dallas, Texas:

"I hardly know what to say. They have just told me that I am liable to execution. I can hardly believe it . . . I am a prisoner of war and I thought I would be taken care of until the end of the war . . . I did everything that the Japanese have asked me to do and tried to cooperate with them because I knew that my part in the war was over." He added that "I wanted to be a commercial pilot and would have been if it hadn't been for this war" and asked his mother to "try and stand up under this and pray."

The next morning, preparations for the coming execution got under way at nearby Public Cemetery No. I. Tomoicha Yoneya was in charge of a detail that erected three small wooden crosses that had been made of new lumber in the regimental carpenter shop the night before along with three wooden boxes. Shigeji Mayawa cut the grass down in the area and helped set up a small table to be used as a ceremonial altar in the tradition of the Knights of the Bushido.

Shortly after four o'clock that afternoon, the three gaunt Americans were hand-cuffed, loaded into separate trucks under heavy guard and taken to the cemetery. Weak and quivering, each was led to one of the wooden crosses, turned around and made to kneel down.

While these preparations were being made, a nine-man rifle squad arrived under the command of 1st Lt. Goro Tashida. He posted three men around the area as security guards and marched the other six into a double rank about twenty feet in front of the three helpless Americans. Two riflemen were assigned to each man — one primary marksman who would fire first, and a secondary in case the first missed or had a misfire.

By this time other Japanese had arrived. The regulations had to be followed to the letter. Accordingly, Colonel Akimobu Ito, prosecutor for the district in which the trial had taken place, Major Itsuro Hata, prosecutor for the case against the accused, Sergeant Sotojiro Tatsuta, prison warden, and Chosei Fujita, clerk of the court when the men were tried, were all present. Three medical officers, members of the Shanghai Military Police Headquarters and an interpreter were also witnesses. When the last required man arrived, an incense burner was lighted on the altar-like table behind the firing squad. All was now in readiness.

Major Hata read a statement condemning the men to death which was interpreted. He then made a few remarks "to make them feel more easy about their coming death." When the interpreter completed the translation, Hata made a deep bow and then allowed the prison warden, Tatsuta, to say a few words. Tatsuta, in his post-war trial testimony, recalled what he said:

> ". . . I told the fliers, 'I do not know what relation I had with you in the previous life but we have been living together under the same roof and on this day you are going to be executed, but I feel sorry for you. Your lives were very short but your names will remain everlastingly. I do not remember if this was Lieutenant Farrow but one of them said, 'Thank you very much for all the trouble you have taken while we were in your confinement, but please tell the folks at home that we died very bravely.' And I told them that 'your ashes will be sent through the International Red Cross to your homes.'
>
> "I told them that Christ was born and died on the cross and you on your part must die on the cross but when you are executed — when you die on the cross you will be honored as Gods, and I told them to pray and they made a sign which resembled the sign of the cross and they prayed. I told them 'you will soon be bound to the crosses and when this is done it is a fact that it is a form that man's faith and cross shall be united. Therefore, have faith.' Then they smiled and said they understood very well. Then I asked them if they had any more to say and they said they had nothing more to say."

When Tatsuta had finished the arms of the men were tied to the crosses. Blindfolds were put over their eyes and a dab of black ink placed on the cloth directly in the center of their foreheads.

Lieutenant Tashida called his men to attention.

"Face the target!" he commanded. The six men turned their bodies toward the three prisoners. Tashida withdrew his saber and raised it above his head.

"Prepare!"

The three soldiers in the front rank raised their rifles, snapped the bolts in place and aimed at the black marks on the blindfolds.

Tashida raised his arm.

"Fire!" he shouted as he snapped his arm down.

Three shots split the afternoon stillness. Each of three bullets smashed squarely into the ink mark targets. The heads of the three men snapped back from the impact simultaneously and then slumped forward. Blood gushed through the blindfolds and covered the ground.

The three medical officers, after a nod from Tashida, rushed forward to check the pulses of the three men. One by one they looked toward Tashida and shook their heads. Death for all three prisoners had been mercifully instantaneous; no second shots were necessary.

While the medical officers bound the wounds, Tashida about-faced his men, marched them a few steps away and ordered them to extract their cartridges. The three coffins were brought forward; the bodies were untied and placed inside by the guards. The coffins were then carried to the altar table where the incense was burning and laid carefully side by side on the ground. In keeping with the ritual according to the Code of the Knights of the Bushido, the entire assemblage stood on the other side of the altar with caps off and heads bowed. After a moment of quiet meditation, the group put their caps on, saluted the coffins and departed. The formalities required under Japanese military law had begun at 1630 hours. By 1720 there was no evidence of what had taken place. It had taken just fifty minutes to retaliate in blood for shattering the myth of invincibility that had been fomented by the Japanese militarists.

The bodies of Hallmark, Farrow, and Spatz were taken to the Japanese Resident's Association Crematorium and promptly cremated. The ashes were placed in small boxes which were tagged and brought back to the waiting room outside the main office of Kiangwan prison. There they were placed on an altar and incense burners lighted and placed in front of them. About a month later the boxes were taken to the International Funeral Home in downtown Shanghai where they remained until the end of the war.

Now six men—Faktor, Dieter, Fitzmaurice, Hallmark, Farrow, and Spatz—had died as a result of participating in the first air raid on the Japanese homeland. But still another of Doolittle's raiders would soon join their ranks.

Barr, DeShazer, Hite, Meder, and Nielsen were unaware that their buddies had been led away never to be seen again. Still in solitary confinement, each was assessing what had happened earlier that day. About 9 o'clock in the morning, they had been permitted to wash themselves. It was a foggy, overcast day that seemed strangely ominous. Chase Nielsen had the feeling that it might be his last day on earth:

"I don't know why I had a strange feeling of foreboding unless it was the sight of some Chinese prisoners carrying shovels. I had heard that the Japanese made prisoners dig their own graves before they were executed and I wondered if these prisoners were going to dig ours as well. The fact that we had been allowed to wash also made me apprehensive. But what really alarmed me was when a squad of guards dressed in their best uniforms and armed with rifles and sabers took us out of our cells one by one.

"I learned later that each of us had the same feeling of impending death. It was a strange thing but all of us had decided individually that we would try to make a break for it if they were taking us away for execution. We figured we might not make it but we were determined to get a guard or two in the process. Each of us had jammed the only possible weapon he possessed in his pocket—a toothbrush. I figured I would jam mine right into a guard's face to start the break.

"We were marched into another building about 50 yards away. But there were only five of us. Farrow and Spatz were missing and we knew they had been in their cells the day before. We hadn't seen Dean Hallmark for over two months and he wasn't there, either. My stomach tightened as we were led into the same courtroom where we had had our farcical trial weeks before. Now I knew that something was going to happen."

There were about fifteen Japanese Army officers jammed into the room, all staring impassively at the bearded, bedraggled Americans. It seemed like a repeat performance of the August trial with the bewigged judges sitting behind the raised dais.

When the Americans were lined up, the chief judge nodded to an interpreter standing nearby. With perspiration streaming down his face, he began to translate laboriously from the Japanese characters on the sheaf of papers he held in his shaking hands.

"It has been proven beyond all doubt," he said, "that the defendants, motivated by a false sense of glory, carried on indiscriminate bombing of schools and hospitals and machine gunned innocent civilians with complete disregard for the rules of war. . . ."

The five prisoners were stunned. Not a gun on either plane had been fired over the target and both bombardiers had dropped their bombs squarely on purely military targets.

". . . The tribunal finds the defendants guilty of violating Sections 1 and 2 of Article 2 of the Military Law concerning the Punishment of Enemy Airmen. . . ."

The prisoners tensed and crouched a little. Instinctively, the guards gripped their rifles tightly and the officers' hands moved toward their sabers.

". . . Therefore, the military tribunal has passed judgment and imposes sentences under the provisions of Article 3 of that law."

The room fell silent as the interpreter paused, wiped the sweat from his brow and coughed nervously. He acted as though the next words were illegible and then continued hesitantly.

". . . The tribunal, acting under the law . . . hereby . . . sentences the defendants . . . to . . . death!"

Nielsen strained at his handcuffs and leaned forward. A guard leveled his rifle at Nielsen's midriff. The others stood at attention as if in a daze. But there was more to come. The interpreter had more lines to deliver.

". . . but, through the graciousness of His Majesty, the Emperor, your sentences are hereby commuted to life imprisonment . . . with special treatment."

The interpreter, obviously relieved at having finished his chore, stepped behind the guards who now formed a solid ring around the five prisoners. At a nod from the chief judge, each prisoner was surrounded and marched back to his cell. The whole procedure had taken less than five minutes. They now had a lifetime to ponder their "crimes" and be thankful for the Emperor's graciousness.

While the five scrawny men languished in the deadly monotony of their solitary confinement, there was one ray of sunshine that penetrated the gloom of their despair. It was the presence of Caesar Luis dos Remedios, their fellow prisoner who had been made a trusty. Remedios, a man of slight build with a large head, felt an unusual compassion for the Americans. He knew how much the Doolittle raid on Tokyo had affected the Japanese and he deeply admired the Americans for their bravery. He gradually proved that he was a true friend and not a stool pigeon for his captors.

Two days after their sentence had been announced, Tatsuta, the prison warden, ordered the men into the prison yard. Through Remedios, he told the Americans again that they had been adjudged as war criminals for bombing, strafing and killing innocent Japanese. The Americans, blinking in the sunlight, wondered why Tatsuta was telling them the same thing all over again. Tatsuta spoke more Japanese and Remedios turned back to the Americans with tears in his eyes.

"The warden says that because of your crime," Remedios said. choked with emotion, "you are sentenced to death."

The five men stared at Remedios in disbelief. Each of them looked toward the 10-foot prison wall and wondered what his chances would be to scale it.

Tatsuta sensed something was wrong with their reactions and asked Remedios what he had said. After a few minutes of conversation, Remedios smiled and said that he had misunderstood; the Americans' lives were spared and they were to serve life sentences instead. Tatsuta then asked the men to be good prisoners and not to try an escape. If they did, he would have no alternative but to have them shot.

Tatsuta then led the men back to the courtroom where they had had their "trial" and let them go through their belongings and take them back to their cells. The jackets and personal effects belonging to Farrow, Hallmark and Spatz were there and the others wondered what had happened to them. "It was obvious to each of us that they had been killed," Hite recalled, "but we didn't dare let each other down. In the few minutes we had together we managed to whisper some theories as to what had happened to them without mentioning our greatest fears. We all knew in our hearts they were gone but we knew it didn't help our morale a bit to admit it."

That afternoon they were allowed to wash their underwear and shirts and take baths. From then on they were allowed a bath once a week. Their heads and beards were clipped regularly. This helped their morale considerably but it was Remedios who did the most to buoy the men's spirits and enable them to keep their hopes up.

In order to disguise his identity, it was decided to refer to Remedios as "Tom" whenever they had the chance to mention his name. He became the communications link between them. He served them their meals three times a day and as he slid the food bowls through the slot in the bottom of each door he would slip a note in all wadded up as if he were shooting marbles. Although a guard was always standing over him, he was never caught.

The risk "Tom" was taking was deeply appreciated by the five men starving for contact with the outside world. The notes were terse but always contained a hopeful message such as "Japanese newspaper says big naval battle fought off Midway Island. I think they lost" and "War will soon be over. You will go home soon." He smuggled the lead taken from pencils he had stolen in to each man and asked them to write down their addresses, dates of birth and other personal information. He promised that he would try to get word out that the men were there. As he reached inside each cell for the bowls, they would slip the wad of paper between his fingers and he would palm it as he withdrew his hands. Although Remedios could never get the word out to friendly contacts, the hope that he engendered in the minds of the Americans was worth the risk and the effort. Their morale soared every time he slipped them a note. Whenever he missed, they felt a deep disappointment and bitter frustration.

The days came and went and each man began to feel the effects of being alone 23½ hours a day. The biggest thing in their lives was the half hour or less they would be let out of their cells for washing and exercise each day. It was reassuring to see the other men and know they were still there. When the guards weren't paying attention, they could talk to each other rapidly—each trying to give the other some hopeful message because they knew instinctively that their lives depended on their mental outlook and faith in their ultimate freedom. But it was the being alone with their own thoughts so much each day that was hard to take. Bob Hite describes what they did to pass the time and preserve their sanity:

"Our cells were horribly cold as the winter came on. The two blankets were not enough on the bare floor and we begged for more. We worried about the simplest of creature comforts frequently but most of those endless days and nights were spent thinking. We examined every little detail of our lives that we could recall. Most of the memories were pleasant—like the things we did as kids, our families, school days, friends, the little everyday things we all take so for granted when we are living out in the world of people. Then we'd think about our personal shortcomings and wondered if we would ever again have the chance to do anything about them.

"Sometimes I wondered how long I could live with myself. There didn't seem to be much depth to me and I got pretty tired of myself and everything about me. I regretted not having done more with my life so that I would be a better companion to myself. Gradually, however, the cold became so intense we couldn't even think. We complained bitterly to the guards and Tom every chance we got. Finally, on December 5, 1942, Tom managed to convince Captain Tatsuta, the warden, that we would die if he didn't do something. With no prior notice we were all herded into one big cell and given three blankets each."

As before, there was a special medicine in just being together. The suddenness of it was almost too much as the five of them jabbered excitedly when the guards slammed the door and shoved the wooden crossbar into place. They didn't know how long their good fortune would last or how long the guards would let them talk.

For about a week the men talked and talked about anything and everything that came to their minds. This time it was different from the time they had been together in Bridge House. They were all in bad physical shape now, having lost much weight from the meager, unbalanced diet. Each man, according to his own metabolism, was experiencing the first symptoms of beri-beri, a serious disease affecting the nerves which is common in areas of the world where polished rice is a staple food. Chief symptoms of the disease are the inability to concentrate, muscle and joint pains, irritability, lack of a sense of well-being and lack of coordination. All five of them had all of these symptoms in varying degrees.

It was Bob Hite who first exhibited the irritability that is so common in all diet-deficient diseases. He was, as he later described, "testy" and unable to control his temper. He would take offense to whatever was said and almost came to blows with anyone who challenged his remarks. Fearful that Hite was cracking up, the other four were careful not to antagonize him.

Bob Meder, the recognized intellectual of the group, seemed to recognize what the poor diet was doing to them all. He instituted a number of games to flex their minds such as spelling bees, contests to name the state capitals, the Presidents, historic dates and anything he could think of to keep their minds active and alert. Chase Nielsen recalled Meder's ingenuity:

"Since food was constantly on our minds, Bob dreamed up a lottery where we would trade food to each other. For instance, we would draw numbers and the winner would trade half a bowl of rice for a bowl of soup or some other fractional distribution. We would be trading back and forth according to his rules so that you might wind up with two bowls of rice for your dinner or two bowls of soup. We also drew lots to see in what order we would take the bowls as they were shoved through the door. All this was exciting to us at the time and it kept us busy trying to keep track, of who owed what to whom. We would use the calcium buttons from our shirts to keep score on the cement walls.

"Bob also devised another game which we played with great gusto. It was what we called the 'flea-lice catch' and we would play it every Sunday morning. We piled all fifteen of the blankets in the middle of the floor and would take one and spread it open. We would then sit around the blanket and at a signal try to catch the fleas and lice as they were revealed. You got only one point for each louse caught because they were an easy-to-see white and didn't move so fast. But you got five points for each black flea, because they were about the size of a pinhead and it took real skill to pin one down. We slowly unfolded the blankets, hunting for "points" until all fifteen were finished. The winner would get a portion of the next meal from the four losers, plus the privilege of picking which bowl he wanted from the five as they were served."

There were many other schemes to divert their minds. To overcome the monotony they changed their positions in the cell each week. They would sit three along one wall and two along the opposite wall next to the smelly *benjo*. The job of receiving the food from the guards and passing it to the others and the collecting of cups, bowls and chopsticks was rotated. After several weeks of this, however, their minds refused to take the mental challenges and their bodies began to cry out with the deepening ravages of the increased malnutrition.

It was January 25, 1943, that the first chink in their physical armor showed up. George Barr had just marked the day on the calendar he was keeping on the wall. Bob Hite was doing pushups trying to reach the goal of 25 he had set for himself. As he reached the twentieth, he felt the sensation that something had snapped in his head and he fell flat on his face. He had passed out cold and when he came to several minutes later he had double vision and couldn't move.

The other fellows yelled to a guard who summoned a medical orderly. The medic gave Hite a shot that put him to sleep for 48 hours. When he came to, Barr, Nielsen and DeShazer had been moved out and he and Meder were alone. For the next ten days Meder fed him at meal times, kept blankets over him and kept talking to keep up his morale.

"Meder had the darndest theories about how the war was progressing," Hite said, "and he'd keep up a monologue all day long. He would piece together bits of information he had gotten from the Japanese newspaper stories through Tom and speculate on what was really happening. We knew that American forces were working their way up the Solomons. The guards would tell us gleefully of the heavy losses of the Americans—several aircraft carriers, so many destroyers, etc. We'd always say that was too bad for us but good for the Japanese. Little by little, though, Meder would point out to me that we were certainly getting closer and closer to Japan despite our 'heavy losses.' Whatever was happening it was good to hear Meder's reasoning. By the time they let the other fellows back in the cell, I was in better mental and physical shape.

"One curious aftermath of my illness was the terrific appetite I developed. I used all sorts of persuasion and finally one of the guards agreed to try to buy some bread and strawberry jam for me with the few American dollar bills I had. The other boys were all glad to see me get it because I must have weighed about 100 lbs. by then. But after about two weeks of these extra rations there seemed to be a resentment building up. It must have been extremely difficult for them to be eating their rice while I ate bread and jam—something they wanted as badly as I did. We finally talked it over and decided that for one meal a day, the extra rations would go to one of the others. After about two weeks the treat stopped and we were back to the usual diet."

Remedios continued to keep their spirits up with his gossipy notes. On February 14th, he flipped a Valentine greeting inside and on April 6th, a birthday greeting to George Barr. He had also obtained a couple of books, among which was a book entitled *Difficulties, or An Attempt to Help*, by Seymour Hicks, an Englishman. It was a humorous book and the men practically memorized it.

One bit of news that Remedios brought them was the fact that there were other Americans in another part of the prison. "Their names are Commander Cunningham and a Corporal Battles," Remedios told them. "They were captured at Wake Island but they have been sent to Kiangwan because they had escaped from jail at Woosung." Remedios had been able to pass a message to Cunningham that five of the Doolittle raiders were also there. It was to be Commander Winfield Scott Cunningham, commander of Wake Island during its heroic last stand, who would help arrange for the release of the Doolittle raid survivors over two years later.*

As suddenly as their stay at Kiangwan had begun, it ended. On April 17, 1943, the five of them were marched into the exercise yard where they were blindfolded and handcuffed. A rope was placed around their waists and then tied to a guard. They were taken to the airport, loaded aboard a passenger plane and handcuffed to their seats. Guards sat on both sides of each prisoner and one behind.

In a part of the world where anniversaries carry special significance, the five Americans were suddenly afraid that their captors were planning to "celebrate" a special day that they would long remember but would like to forget. The next day would be exactly one year since sixteen B-25 Mitchell bombers had lifted off the deck of the *Hornet* on a day that historians were to mark as the high noon of the Japanese Empire. The five Americans, doomed to life imprisonment with "special treatment," marked the end of their first year as "War Criminals." Their destination: Nanking. Their fate: Unknown.

---

*Contrary to popular belief, Cunningham was in command of the forces on Wake and not Major James P. S. Devereux, USMC, who was widely acclaimed as a hero after the war. Devereux was alleged to have replied when the Navy asked him what he needed, "Send us more Japs!" Such a message was never sent.

7

TWO MORE YEARS OF HELL

*T*HE FLIGHT TO NANKING lasted about an hour. Although they were not told what the city was, both Barr and Nielsen, being navigators, recalled the landmarks on their charts they had studied so long aboard the *Hornet*. In spite of their blindfolds, they could see under them out the uncurtained windows.

It was one of the curious inexplicables of their captivity that whenever they were being transported from one place to another, they were always well treated. The guards became more considerate and offered them cigarettes. It was a welcome respite but it was short-lived. When they landed they were whisked to the new military prison recently completed to take care of the increasing number of Chinese prisoners. Bob Hite tells of his reactions as the blindfolds were taken off:

"We were pleasantly surprised at our new 'accommodations.' Everything was new and after some of the filthy places we had been in, it was like moving from a tenement in the slums to a *House and Garden* model home.

"As we walked down the corridor of one cell block, we counted twelve cells in all and wondered who else would be there. They lined us up by size and put Barr in No. 1 and Nielsen in 2 because these cells were larger than the others. Meder was put in 3, me in 4 and DeShazer, shortest of us all, in 5. They then gave us the Japanese equivalent of these numbers and told us we were to answer to these whenever we were called instead of our names which the Japanese found hard to pronounce.

"The cells were about ten feet square and dark because the window was near the ceiling so that we couldn't see out. We were back in solitary confinement which we detested but there were compensations. After about a month we had some furniture moved in — a desk and a chair. But they were nailed to the floor so we didn't have the pleasure of arranging our 'rooms' to suit our tastes. But it was good to sit in a chair again — a luxury I never thought of until it had been denied. We still had to sleep on the floor, however."

There were other luxuries the men were to enjoy at Nanking. The food was slightly more plentiful, although it was still dirty rice and tea spiced occasionally with unidentified floating objects and pieces of meat in a soupy mixture to break the monotony. Each man had four blankets which were relatively new. Best of all, the prison was so new that lice, fleas and rats had not yet found it. Their lack was a comfort they had not believed possible.

But the prospect of more long, lonely hours in solitary confinement was a shattering one. They had lost their friend "Tom" Remedios. Whether they could ever find another "Tom" to replace him was doubtful. The *cordon sanitaire* their captors had erected for them as part of their "special treatment" was complete. No one ever occupied the other seven cells. The only concession made by the Japanese to the five prisoners was a daily exercise period of fifteen minutes each day in the courtyard. They had had so little sunlight for over a year that they were all as white as alabaster. One of the odd things they noticed about each other was the clear, sparkling whiteness of their eyes. As Meder remarked, "Maybe it's our clean living that gives us clear eyes; doing nothing has one compensation anyhow."

There was another ray of morale-building hope in the exercise period other than the chance to be together and exchange a few words when the guards weren't listening. Shortly after their first exercise period, one of the Japanese guards lined them up and introduced himself by saying, "Me Sportsman!" He was what Bob Hite called a "happy Jap," one of the few they ever saw. He had a competitive spirit and challenged the five Americans — all taller than he was — to wrestle with him one at a time while the other guards looked on. Although the prisoners were extremely weak, their greater size was sometimes too much for the Sportsman. But each time he won, he would shout happily, "Nippon Banzai! Nippon Banzai! ("Japan wins! Japan wins!") And each time he won, the Americans noticed slightly more food at the next meal. When this was confirmed by experimentation and comparing notes between them it was unanimous that Japan would have the honor of beating the United States at their junior Olympics from then on although they would all put on a good act to please their opponent.

The exercise period and the few minutes they were allowed to wash each day were the only times the five fliers were allowed out of their cells. The rest of the time they paced their cells restlessly. While they all remained weak throughout the summer, they did not feel that their physical conditions were declining further. It was their mental condition that slowly began to deteriorate, however. They began to have hallucinations based on their basic human needs. They had "mirages" as they stared at the walls and imagined that they saw huge plates of meat, vegetables and desserts. They reviewed in their minds the things they had done in their childhood that had given them pleasure. They began to "see" the faces of friends and relatives etched on the ceiling when they would lie down. They recalled pleasant memories consistently; none of them can remember thinking of unpleasant things that may have happened to them. Their reveries got longer in duration. They actually resented it when they were broken by the guards sliding open the slot at the bottom of their doors to shove food in or the upper one to peer in and check on what the prisoners were doing.

Since they had nothing new to stimulate their minds, each began to "create" by mental imagery. Nielsen mentally built a home from the ground up after first deciding on his floor plan and layout of the lot he recalled wanting to buy someday in his hometown in Utah. He mentally dug the basement, constructed the framework and nailed the shingles on the roof. Then he carefully covered the framework, brick by brick, and started on the interior. He decided on color schemes and even bathroom fixtures. Landscaping came next and finally he was through. The mental exercise had been exhilarating but also frustrating because when he had finished "building" his dream house there was once again the nothingness of the lonely cell.

The others gave themselves similar mental tasks to pass the hundreds of lonely hours away. Barr worked mentally on an elaborate neon sign while Hite planned a model farm from the clearing of the land to the sinking of the last fence post. DeShazer composed poetry on a mental blackboard which he would "erase" until he found the proper rhyming words to express the thought he was searching for. Meder reviewed books he had read years before and composed philosophical essays. He would recite poetry he had memorized in high school and make mental outlines of the classics he had enjoyed in his formative years.

The summer faded rapidly in Nanking in 1943 and with the fall came the ominous feeling that they might not survive a hard winter in their weakened condition. The unheated cells, their lowered resistance and the complete lack of medical attention would probably mean an easy susceptibility to respiratory diseases. But there was nothing they could do except worry about it—and pray.

During the last week of September, Bob Meder developed a bad case of dysentery. He had severe attacks about three times a day which increased to five times a day over the next two weeks. Although already seriously underweight, he rapidly lost more pounds and became so weak he could not exercise although he did manage to get outside and exchange a few words with the others each day. In spite of his prolonged battle, Meder kept his sense of humor and never let the others know how miserable he felt. He remained cheerful but it was easy to see that he would not survive if he did not get medical attention.

One of the guards, nicknamed "Cyclops" because of his thick glasses, liked Meder and seemed genuinely concerned about his deteriorating health. He had long talks with Meder in his broken English. They tutored each other in Japanese and English through the slit in Meder's cell door when the other guards were not around.

By the end of November, Meder's legs began to swell which was the first outward sign of beri-beri. Although he continued to smile and joke, he must have known his days were numbered without medical attention. He reminded Nielsen during an exercise period that they had promised each other to visit the families of any of them who did not survive their imprisonment. Nielsen was alarmed because it was not at all like Meder to make a remark that was not happily optimistic.

"Meder was sitting on the steps outside the cell building when he said that," Nielsen recalled, "and he had said it to me because I was the nearest one to him. I walked over to him and asked him how he felt. He said that he was really sick and asked me to say a prayer for him."

The corporal in charge of the guard detail that day was one of the meanest and most sadistic of the prison detachment. As soon as he saw Nielsen talking to Meder he shouted at the pair to stop talking.

Nielsen paid no attention and began to talk as rapidly as he could to Meder. He could see now that Meder was dangerously ill. The more the guard yelled, the more determined Nielsen was to keep talking. The other guards quickly ushered Barr, DeShazer and Hite to their cells. Nielsen calmly lifted Meder to his feet and helped him down the hallway toward his cell. By this time the chief guard was livid with rage. As Nielsen passed him, the guard lashed out with his fist and caught Nielsen squarely in the face.

Nielsen staggered under the blow but kept his temper. He let go of Meder, calmly put down the bucket he was carrying in the other hand and paused. With all the strength he could muster, Nielsen snapped his right fist forward and caught the guard flush on the jaw, knocking him against the wall. The other guards were surprised and sucked air between their teeth as all Japanese do when something unusual occurs.

Stunned and humiliated, the guard recovered and tried to strike back at Nielsen with his steel sword scabbard. Each time he lashed out with it, Nielsen dodged in a fighting crouch. Since there wasn't much room in the narrow hallway, the guard could not get a full swing and never did land any blows but struck several of the other guards. Nielsen wondered if his adversary was going to pull his sword out of the scabbard but he never did. After a few minutes the guard withdrew and Nielsen, the obvious victor, was led to his cell fully expecting to receive some severe punishment for his defiance. To his surprise, the guard was seen only one more time and the affair must have been forgotten. From that time on when any guards would push or shove Nielsen, all he had to do was drop into a fighting crouch and the guards would back up a respectful distance.

A few minutes after the five men were in their cell, Meder called Cyclops, the friendly guard, to his cell door and asked him partly in English and partly in Japanese, if he would see that his personal belongings would be sent to his family in the States if he should die. Bob Hite, in the next cell, overheard the conversation and asked Cyclops to get a doctor for Meder.

Later that day a military doctor, Lt. Soshi Yasuharu, gave Meder an injection of vitamin B and made several subsequent visits. But the weeks of dysentery and poor diet could not be overcome by cursory treatment. By December 11, 1943, the once strong and healthy track star had reached the limits of his physical endurance. That afternoon he staggered out to the steps during the exercise period and managed his usual smile. The others each spoke a few words of encouragement to him before they returned to their cells.

At supper time that evening, George Barr was given the "privilege" of being let out of his cell to shove the food bowls through the door to the other prisoners. When he shoved Meder's bowl in and spoke a few words there was no answer. Barr called the guard who sent Barr back to his cell then opened Meder's door and found Meder's lifeless body sprawled on the floor. The gallant pilot became the seventh member of Doolittle's crews to die as a result of the Tokyo Raid.

The guards summoned Lt. Yasuharu who confirmed that the American was dead. Fearing possible reprisals from his superiors, he rushed back to his office and wrote the following false medical report:

MEDICAL REPORT ON
SECOND LIEUTENANT ROBERT J. MEDER

Nature of Disease: Heart failure resulting from beri-beri and inflammation of the intestines.

Record of Condition: At the beginning of October, 1943, the patient began to lose appetite and had sticky muddy excrements from two to three times a day.

Given medicine for the stomach to arrest dysentery and beri-beri, but the doctor failed to discover any improvement.

On the 18th of October the lower part of the legs began to swell and show the symptoms of beri-beri.

Vitamin B was injected under the skin and a daily dose of glucose was also injected. A hot water bottle was used. This treatment was begun on 26 October and the patient began showing signs of improvement.

On 1 December the patient showed noticeable signs of improvement, took free exercise in the mornings and went to bed in the afternoons.

At 1710 hours December 1, 1943, suddenly the condition changed and the patient's breath stopped. Immediately artificial respiration was tried and 3.0cc of camphor was injected under the skin and 1.0cc of adrenalin was injected into the heart but the patient failed to recover.

Certified by Medical 1st Lt. Soshi Yasuharu
December 1943.

None of the other prisoners knew that Meder had died that day and Barr could not tell them. When they were led out to exercise the next day, they were not allowed to pass his cell. Later they heard hammering and much commotion in his cell. When the noise ceased they were led one by one into his cell and found that a crude wooden coffin had been constructed. Inside, Meder lay in final repose. The guards had placed flowers on his chest. In their simple way they were paying homage to an enemy warrior who had served his country honorably to the end.

After the four survivors had paid their last respects, Meder's body was taken to a nearby funeral parlor and cremated. Next day his ashes were brought back in a small box which was placed in Cell No. 12 across from George Barr along with all of Meder's belongings.

Meder's death was a severe mental blow to his four buddies. In their separate cells they each prayed and recalled how his effervescent sense of humor had sustained them through their year and a half of captivity. They began to worry about their own health and wondered how long it would be before their names would be added to the death roster. During the exercise periods they thought about Meder and wondered why he had to be taken. Their only conclusion was that it was the will of God.

Brooding over Meder's death developed their interest in religion to a greater degree than any of them had thought possible. Their minds were starved for new thoughts. They remarked to each other in the exercise periods how wonderful it would be they had something to read. Finally they got permission from the guards to write a note to the Commandant. In it they pointed out their poor physical condition and asked him to show them some mercy by giving them something to read.

The death of Meder had caused some concern among the Japanese prison officers. By the turn of the year into 1944, it was plainly evident that the Japanese armies were fighting defensively on every front. If Japan should lose the war it was possible that someone might be called to account for the conditions that had caused Meder's death. The warden decided that the Americans should have their wish for books. He sent an orderly into the city to look for religious books in English. He returned with five of them: *The Son of God* by Karl Adams; *The Spirit of Catholicism*, also by Adams; *The Unknown God* by Alfred Noyes, and *The Hand of God*, by

William Scott. A fifth book was given to them which was like the fulfillment of a dream. It was an old English Bible and its message was to have a profound effect on the four survivors.

The books were an overwhelming godsend and an inspiration to them. They passed them back and forth via the guards and virtually memorized them. And out of the hours of concentrated reading about Christianity they each developed their own religious philosophy which helped sustain them in the darker days ahead. They each concluded that they had no real hatred for the guards, vicious and mean as they were. The Bible's passages of faith, hope, and charity got through to them all. Their attitude, morale and outlook improved as they read the age-old verses with new understanding.

The ensuing days of solitary confinement passed like a gray blur, punctuated here and there with incidents that either terrified, enraged or saddened them. But there were also occasions when incidents gladdened them, too. One day during meal time, Nielsen happened to turn his aluminum cup over and found some writing on the bottom. The writing said "Connie G. Battles, U.S. Marines."

Nielsen could hardly contain himself until the next exercise period. As soon as he could whisper to the others he told them what he had found. For the first time they knew that there were other Americans in the prison. Nielsen told how he had rubbed out Battles' name and had scratched his own in its place with a nail he had found in his cell. Thus began the Tincup News Service.

The drinking cup went from cell to cell and finally got back to Battles in his section, of the prison. Battles had been in a civilian internment camp in Shanghai and had learned a lot of news of the outside world that they had not heard of. Soon one of the four Doolittle men found another message on the bottom of a cup. It read: "Russians on German border." This was scratched off to let Battles know they had received it and another message put in its place about the Doolittle raiders.

During the exercise periods the four Doolittle raiders agreed to each take a section of their story and tell it in increments on their respective utensils. They scratched their names, serial numbers, squadron designations, dates of their capture, and anything else they could think of that would identify them. They all worried about what would happen to them at the end of the war and wanted to let other Americans know that the four of them were still alive.

In return, the Doolittle men learned that Commander W. S. Cunningham, Commander of Wake Island when it fell, Battles, and five other Americans were in an adjoining cell block. They had attempted an escape and had been recaptured. As punishment, they were confined in the same military prison because they were considered "dangerous."*

---

*The full account of the Wake Island battle and the capture and imprisonment of Commander Cunningham and his men can be found in *Wake Island Command* by W. Scott Cunningham with Lydel Sims (Boston: Little, Brown, 1961).

This method of communication was slow and sketchy but it did more to keep them sane and full of hope than anything else besides the Bible. But like everything else in their prison lives, the Tincup News Service was discovered and came to an abrupt end. For days after that the four Doolittle fliers were slapped and kicked by the guards at the slightest provocation and though they often struck back, they always came out second best because their reflexes were extremely slow and they never saw the first blow coming.

After the news service was broken up, they relied on a Morse code system between cells that Meder had worked out before his death. A rap on the cell wall was a dot and a scratch for a dash. Since all had taken code in their flying training, it was just a matter of reviewing the alphabet and using it. Never had any of them imagined when they struggled with it in ground school that they would use it as a means of communication through prison walls. Since being able to communicate their thoughts to one another was a vital requirement for their hungry minds, they all became very proficient. It was this system plus the daily exercise periods that sustained them and enabled each to check on the well-being of the other.

The weeks inched by and the winter became spring. Although the weather had been cold and damp, none of the four weakening prisoners caught a respiratory disease, for which they were thankful. But as the days lengthened and the spring became summer, the heat proved to be as great a discomfort as the cold had been.

Meteorologists have recorded that the summer of 1944 was the hottest in Nanking's history. The four Americans in their solitary cells can only attest that they have never been hotter in their lives for such an extended period of time. There was no circulation of air. The cell doors were solid and the two small slots were always closed except when the guards chose to open them to inspect or shove in food. The tiny window was so high that there was no chance to get near it to get a breath of fresh air. They felt like pieces of meat being slowly roasted in their wooden ovens.

Bob Hite developed a severely high fever in the middle of the summer and was near death. When the guards saw that his life was ebbing away, they removed the wooden door and replaced it with a screen door.

The death of Meder had caused some concern among the prison officials and now another of the Doolittle prisoners was dying. The war was going badly for the Japanese on all fronts by this time in spite of official propaganda to the contrary. What if the Allies should capture Nanking and learn that two of the Doolittle Raiders had died because of poor medical treatment? Would not the Americans someday seek revenge?

The records do not show the "why" of it, but a medical assistant was ordered to live in the prison and nurse Hite back to health. He gave Hite shots, sponge baths and extra food rations. Under this kind of benevolent attention and with the advent of cooler weather as the summer faded, Hite recovered. It was a relief to his three buddies to have him rejoin them in the exercise yard. Their prayers had been answered. The Bible's message of hope and faith had newer meaning now.

The winter of 1944–45 shared the same statistical honor as the previous summer— the worst on record. Snow fell on December 1 and stayed on the ground until March 1. Heavier clothes were issued to the prisoners and, as the weather became more severe, they were given their own American uniforms back which were now so large they put them on over their prison garb.

A memorable day during the long winter was Christmas Day, 1944. While the four men huddled in their cells wondering what their loved ones were doing that day on the other side of the world, they heard the unmistakable roar of airplane engines. Straining to see the small patch of sky allotted to them through the cell window, some strange fighter planes roared over the prison headed for a group of oil storage tanks and a refinery nearby. The angry snarl of the fighters was followed by bomb explosions and machine gun fire. Black smoke billowed slowly skyward and blotted out the sun. Nanking was being bombed! What a Christmas present!

The four Americans cheered loudly when they realized what had happened. Those were new American fighter planes they had never seen before. Surely more would come and the war would soon be over. Their hopes soared but they listened and waited in vain. The skies were silent as the hours turned into days and the days into weeks with no other hopeful signs of coming victory.

The possibility of an eventual Allied victory did not deter the Japanese guards from harassment of their prisoners whenever it occurred to them. George Barr, tallest of the prisoners and a center of attraction to the guards because of his brilliant red hair and beard, was the recipient of many extra pushes, punches and shoves. His worst torture took place in January, 1945, during an exercise period:

"We wore cumbersome slippers whenever we went outside which always fell off as we jogged around the yard. It was always easier to take them off and run in our bare feet—even in the snow. Normally we were allowed to wash our feet in a pail of water afterward.

"I was used to being singled out by the guards for something extra and I always managed to keep my temper. But I had my limits and one of the guards exceeded them when, instead of letting me wash my feet in water one day, he ordered me to wash them in the snow instead. I refused and started back to my cell.

"Without warning the guard struck me on the legs with his sword. I saw red. I whirled around and smashed him a good one right in the nose. He went down and the other guards rushed over to help him. I was weak but the Japanese don't know how to use their fists. I managed to land a few good rights before I was overpowered by the sheer weight of numbers.

"They dragged me back out to the exercise yard and held me down while they slipped a strait jacket around my body. Two of them put their feet on me and tugged at the laces until it was so tight I gasped for breath. They put a rope through my arms at the elbows and tied it securely in the back. All I could move was my legs.

"There was no pain at first, only the agony of trying to get one breath of air. Then the pain began. I felt an unmanageable panic I had never known when I tried to breathe. I could hear myself making animal-like noises and I thought my head was going to burst. There was an enormous pressure behind my eyeballs and in my nostrils. I was sure that I was going to die and I fought hysterically for the precious gift of air.

"While I struggled vainly on the ground, the guards stood around grinning. One of them had a watch. By the end of a half hour I found that my struggles had loosened the laces slightly and I could inhale and exhale in short gasps. The horrible pain turned to numbness and I felt like I was going to die from the constriction of the blood vessels in my head. I tried to scream but that only made things worse.

"At a nod from the guard with the watch, the other guard came over to me and I thought they were going to let me out. Instead, they tightened the laces even more and I thought I was a goner for sure then. It was the same excruciating pain all over again and the panic of not being able to take in or let out even a little gasp.

"I don't know how long a person can last under those conditions but the Japanese guards knew. At the end of the second half hour, the one with the watch nodded and the others came over again. By that time I was so numb with pain my brain had almost stopped working. I knew that if they tightened the jacket once more my life was over.

"Evidently the average person can survive an hour of this kind of torture because instead of tightening the laces, they loosened them and took the jacket off. Never in my life had I valued a breath of air so much. Like everything else free in life, we never realize how sweet the air we breathe is until it is denied.

"I could stand up after all this but I could not take the towel one guard handed me to wipe the perspiration off my face. They led me stumbling back to my cell. One of the guards, one of the two or three friendly ones we ever had, lit and gave me a cigarette—the first I had had in three years. I appreciated the gesture but an hour in the jacket was the most harrowing experience of my life. I'll never forget it."

The spring came early in Nanking in 1945. The lengthening of the days coincided with the increasing daytime temperature. Barr and the others wondered if their bodies and minds could take another torturing summer. Weaker in body and spirit, they prayed that something would happen to break the monotony and spare them from a death that now seemed inevitable.

The "Something" they yearned for took place on June 15, 1945. At 6:30 A.M. the guards took the four men from their cells, handcuffed them and put long robes around them. They then placed hoods over their heads and loaded them aboard a train. Each man had a guard who hung on to a rope tied to their waists.

As before, whenever they had traveled from one place to another, the food was good and plentiful. Blindfolds and handcuffs were taken off at mealtime and the prisoners saw that there were many Japanese officers aboard. They were getting the same meals as the prisoners were, which meant meat and other nourishing solids. Strangely, they were given no water. The combination of the mouth-drying food and the heat caused an almost unbearable thirst. When they complained, a guard who could speak English explained that if they didn't drink, they, the guards, wouldn't have to take them to the latrines. This rationalization almost killed the four prisoners who were sick from the dehydration.

After almost three days of riding, the train finally stopped. They had arrived at the ancient city of Peking, a city of wide boulevards and great squares. As is so true of many Oriental cities, Peking, was a city of paradoxes. It was a city of classic order and culture on the one hand and unbelievable squalor and poverty on the other. It was a city famous for its great wall, built at cost of millions of lives and its Ming tombs, built to memorialize the death of emperors. Under Japanese occupation, it was the headquarters for thousands of Army troops. Its jails were full of Chinese awaiting their fate for crimes they could not comprehend.

To the four Doolittle prisoners, Peking meant a change in their "special treatment." They were placed in an inner section of the military prison in solitary cells and soon discovered that their treatment was not as good as it had gotten to be in Nanking. They were made to sit all day in their cells, on little stools made out of a piece of two-by-four about eight inches long and face the wall three feet away. At night they were given a straw mat to lie on. The meals declined noticeably in quantity and food value. Within a few days, sick with despair, their strength ebbed dangerously low.

Jake DeShazer now became the weakest of the four. He developed huge boils—he counted seventy-five at one time—all over his body. He became delirious and couldn't sit on the stool. When he could no longer respond to the commands of the guard to sit up on the stool, a Japanese medical officer finally gave him vitamin shots until his health improved.

DeShazer, the quiet, mild-mannered Oregonian, was the only enlisted man of the quartet. Never complaining, he had had the same kind of mental torment as the others. From the day he had first gotten hold of the Bible, however, he was a changed man. While all of the men valued the Great Book's words, DeShazer memorized them and recited the verses over and over to himself. Gradually, the words took on deep meaning and significance. His hatred for his captors slowly vanished as he experienced a "revelation" in which he believes that the Lord spoke to him and urged him to show "faith as a grain of mustard seed."

The experiences of prison life that DeShazer had became symbolic and he felt that there was a reason for all of them. If he had the faith that the Bible urged him to have, he became suddenly sure of his eventual release. He describes an episode that encouraged him greatly as he struggled to maintain the faith he had laboriously developed:

"I was being taken back to my cell by one of the guards after a short exercise period one day and the guard started pushing me. 'Hiaku! Hiaku!' (Hurry up! Hurry up!) he shouted, jamming me in the back with his rifle.

"When we came to the door of my cell, he held it open a little and gave me a final push through the doorway. Before I could get all the way in, he slammed the door and caught my foot. He held the door against my bare foot and kicked it with his hobnailed shoes. I pushed against the door to get my foot free and then jumped inside.

"The pain in my foot was severe and I thought some bones were broken. But as I sat on my stool in great pain, I felt as if God were testing me somehow. Instead of hatred and bitterness toward the guard, I remembered the words of Jesus who said, 'Love your enemies, bless them that curse you, do good to them that hate you, and pray for them which despitefully use you, and persecute you.'

"The next morning the same guard came up to the door and opened the slot. When he did, I looked up, smiled and said, 'Ohayoo gozaimasu' (Good morning). The guard looked at me with a puzzled expression, probably thinking that I must have been in solitary too long.

"Several days went by and I tried to make friends with him with my poor knowledge of Japanese. He did not react immediately but, finally, one day he smiled and began to converse. I didn't know much Japanese but I was able to talk to him about his family. Every day after that we exchanged pleasantries and he didn't holler at me when I walked around the cell instead of being seated on the stool. One morning he opened the slot and handed in a boiled sweet potato. I was surprised and thanked him profusely. Later, he gave me some batter-fried fish and candy. I knew then that God's way will work if we really try, no matter what the circumstances."

There was still another episode to come in DeShazer's religious awakening. On August 9, 1945, he awoke as the first ray of sunlight streaked through the morning haze. He heard a voice tell him in clear tones to "start praying":

"I asked, 'What shall I pray about?' Pray for peace and pray without ceasing, I was told. I had prayed about peace but very little, if at all, before that time, as it seemed useless. I thought God could stop the war any time with the power which He had manifested.

"But God was now teaching me the lesson of cooperation. It was God's joy for me to be willing to let Him use me. God does use human instruments to accomplish His will here on earth. It will be a great joy to us through all eternity if we can cooperate with Him. I started to pray for peace although I had a very poor idea of what was taking place in the world at that time.

"About seven o'clock in the morning I began to pray. It seemed very easy to pray on the subject of peace. I prayed that God would put a great desire in the hearts of the Japanese leaders for peace. I thought about the days of peace that would follow. Japanese people would no doubt be discouraged, and I felt sympathetic toward them. I prayed that God would not allow them to fall into persecution by the victorious armies.

"At two o'clock in the afternoon the Holy Spirit told me, 'You don't need to pray any more. The victory is won.' I was amazed. I thought this was quicker and better than the regular method of receiving world news. Probably this news broadcast had not come over the radio to America as yet. I thought I would just wait and see what was to happen."

DeShazer had no way of knowing that August 9, 1945, was the day that the second atomic bomb had been dropped on a Japanese city and that the Japanese were considering complete surrender. The prisoners were told nothing but they could sense something in the air during the next few days. But DeShazer's spirits soared because he *knew* the war was over. He could not help wondering what would happen to Japan now that her dreams of conquest were smashed but he felt that if the defeated Japanese found out about Jesus, the military defeat would be in reality a great victory for the surviving generations.

It was then that DeShazer had a "vision." As he awoke on the morning of August 20th, he was blinded by a brightness so radiant he could not see. A voice, the same one he had heard before, said, "Your travail will soon be over and you will be free. You will return to your loved ones and rejoice once more. But you are called to return to the Japanese people and teach them the way of the Lord."

Later that day a prison guard opened DeShazer's cell door wide and, smiling, beckoned him to come out. "War over," he said. "You go home now."

8
· · · · ·

THREE YEARS, FOUR MONTHS
AND ONE WEEK

*I*T WAS EXACTLY TWO HOURS and forty-five minutes past midnight on August 6, 1945, when Colonel Paul W. Tibbets released the brakes on his B-29, the *Enola Gay*. He roared down the runway of the tiny Pacific atoll named Tinian on a mission that forever altered the course of history. At a quarter after nine in the morning, Major Thomas W. Ferebee, the *Enola Gay*'s bombardier, flipped a toggle switch that released a single bomb on the Japanese city of Hiroshima. That bomb was the most powerful bomb in the world with an explosive force equal to 20,000 tons of TNT. The awesome fireball and the mushroom cloud that followed could be seen 390 miles away.

Sixteen hours after the release of the bomb, President Truman, en route to the United States from the Potsdam Conference, warned the Japanese people that if their leaders did not surrender they might "expect a rain of ruin from the air, the like of which has never been seen on this earth."

In spite of the obliteration of one of their cities by a single bomb dropped from a single American plane, Japanese Army officials played down the significance of what had happened. On August 9th, another B-29 named *Bock's Car* and piloted by Major Charles W. Sweeney, dropped a second atomic bomb, more efficient and destructive than the first, on the city of Nagasaki. At that very moment, the inner Council of the Japanese Government was in session discussing surrender terms. Emperor Hirohito and Premier Kantaro Suzuki had already decided to accept the terms of surrender announced at Potsdam on July 26th. Within a few hours of the second atomic attack, the decision of the cabinet to accept the surrender terms was transmitted to the United States via the Swiss Government. At noon on August 15th, the Japanese people first learned of the surrender through a transcribed radio address by their Emperor.

The hours and days that followed the acceptance of surrender terms were filled with great activity and considerable uncertainty in the headquarters of the Allied Air Forces that had been drawing ever nearer to that inevitable day of victory. While hundreds of American planes kept up a show of force over the home islands, still others were given errands of mercy that contrasted sharply with their recent bombing attacks. Their mission was to locate and supply POW and internee camps until the thousands of U.S. and Allied prisoners could be evacuated.

About 200 POW camps had been located by photo reconnaissance planes. Bombers were converted for their humanitarian missions by the installation of cargo platforms which were parachuted out over the "target" areas. Supplies included food, clothing and 110-pound medical kits with instructions included. Within a few days most of the camps had received their first delivery of clothing, medicine and a three-day stock of food consisting of soups, fruit juices, extracts, vitamins, and other emergency supplies. Unfortunately, these missions were not without cost. Eight aircraft were lost and seventy-seven airmen gave their lives to the effort. In another stroke of irony, a number of prisoners, running out to grab the supplies before they were carried off by the Japanese, were killed by the falling packs.

While the world's attention focused on the negotiations for the formal surrender ceremony, the Commanding General, Army Air Forces, China Theater, had a sudden change of mission. He was required "to assist and advise the Chinese in the rapid occupation of key areas in China and the liberation and rehabilitation of Allied internees and prisoners of war." The Tenth Air Force, based in India and Burma, was given the task which was "equivalent to operating from Los Angeles, California to Halifax, Nova Scotia; from Sitka, Alaska to Mexico City, or from the Hudson Bay to South America."*

In planning to carry out the next assignment, the instructions of the planners were specific in regard to the rescue and evacuation of American and Allied POW's:

Chinese and United States commanders of forces of occupation will take vigorous and immediate action to gain control of Allied Prisoner of War and Internee Camps which may be located within their areas. Such action will be given first priority above all other operations commensurate with the existing situation. Upon acquiring control of Allied Prisoner of War or Internee Camps, there will be conducted an immediate investigation of the conditions under which those camps have operated, and all necessary evidence will be collected and secured to initiate action against any person guilty of criminal negligence or acts against Allied prisoners of war or civilian internees.**

Tenth Air Force Operations in China, Hq., Tenth Air Force, November, 1945 (Doc. 9162-27).
**Japanese Capitulation* (Air Officer Plans), AAFCT, 6 August 1945 (Doc. 9162-21).

By August 15th, arrangements had been made for the dropping of OSS liaison teams into POW camps. Leaflets had been prepared to inform the Japanese of their duties with reference to the release of prisoners and these were dropped along with the POW supplies. Simultaneously, word was flashed to OSS units to alert their personnel for missions into the Jap-held cities while American bomber and transport units began their supply-dropping missions.

The POW camps near Peking and the military prison inside the city were high on the OSS list for liberation. Inside one section of the prison and completely unaware that the war was about to end were a few Americans and several hundred Japanese military prisoners, who had been singled out for "special" treatment. One of the Americans was Commander W. Scott Cunningham, the senior naval officer in command of Wake Island when it was overrun by the Japanese on December 23, 1941. In his book, *Wake Island Command*, he describes his imprisonment in Peking during the few days before he was released:

"The military prison to which we were taken in Peking was in some ways the grimmest of all our places of confinement. The relative informality of the routine at Nanking was replaced by military tautness. Everything was done by bugle calls, and we never got out of our cells except for the morning five-minutes wash. Exercise periods were unheard of; the guards were rough and impatient, and often emphasized their commands with kicks or slaps.

"Using the plate-scratching technique Battles had developed at Nanking, we located the Doolittle flyers here. But again the guards caught on and put a stop to the correspondence.

"On August 13 a change occurred. The usual drills for Japanese prisoners were halted, there were fewer bugle calls, and an unaccustomed stillness pervaded the inside of the prison. Through the cell window we could see feathery ashes floating in the air, ashes we could tell were made by burning paper. Ordinarily paper was never burned in China, for it was too valuable; we deduced the Japanese were burning records, and our spirits soared.

"About noon a guard came to our cell and ordered us to stand at attention. We were not told the reason, but I have since concluded it must have been at the time the Emperor's broadcast accepting the surrender terms was put on the air. That afternoon heavy clothing was thrown into our cell and we could see it was also being issued to the Japanese prisoners. It was an indication we were to be moved to a colder climate, a change we did not welcome. But in a little while the guards returned and the clothing was taken away.

"Then, after all our excitement and high hopes, nothing happened.

"For five days we waited, torn between hope and anxiety. On the morning of August 18 I offered my cellmates a prediction.

" 'Today is the twenty-ninth anniversary of my entry into the Navy.' I said. 'That means there will be developments. Important ones.'

"Like all good soothsayers, I kept my oracle vague. But as the day wore on with no apparent differences from the others, I began to fear even that general prophecy was wrong. I plucked up hope when we were served first instead of last when the evening meal was dished out, and when we discovered the meat was better than any we had had since our arrival. But several more hours passed uneventfully, and when the bugle sounded 'Tattoo' at nine I was ready to give up and settle down for my 1330th night in confinement.

"Then, just as I was on the point of making an open acknowledgment of failure as a fortuneteller, a guard opened our cell door and marched us out.

"We were taken to one of the office rooms in the prison. There the six of us were joined by another survivor of Wake, a civilian named Raymond Rutledge who had been imprisoned in July for trying to escape from a POW camp near Peking. After an hour's wait the prison commandant arrived and made a little speech which was translated by an interpreter.

"It was very brief. 'The war is over,' he said. 'We hope the Americans and the Japanese will shake hands and become friends again. You will be taken from here tonight to another place.'

"Then, turning to me, he said: 'I regret that the furnishings in your room were not better, as you are an officer.'

"I could scarcely restrain a smile. The furnishings in my room consisted of one blackout curtain over the window and a sleeping mat for each inmate.

"The commandant had not said who won the war, but we had no doubts about that. And now that the moment we had dreamed of so long had come, we looked at each other almost in bewilderment.

"We were elated, of course, but there was an element of anticlimax in the elation. We had waited almost too long. And as long as we remained in the power of the Japanese, there was a chance that some fanatic might seize a last opportunity to kill a few enemies of the Emperor."

Commander Cunningham had good reason to fear last-minute retaliation from his captors. After 3½ years of rough treatment, much of it at the hands of Japanese soldiers of low intelligence, who took sadistic delight in taunting the Americans, anything could happen. Knowing this, Tenth Air Force intelligence officers laid on air reconnaissance missions to the known POW camps in conjunction with supply drops. The OSS parachute team, led by Major Ray A. Nichol, dropped into the outskirts of Peking on August 17th.

The actions of this small band of six OSS operatives for the next three days which was covered in the opening chapter is proof of the extent to which brave men will go to save their comrades-in-arms. They had leaped into the midst of thousands of armed Japanese whose conduct, even though they knew of the surrender announcement, would be unpredictable. It took a special kind of courage and Nichol and his men had it. Although armed to the teeth, they could never match the firepower of the enemy soldiers whose officers might not accept the hard fact of surrender. Whatever their personal fears may have been, it is to the eternal credit of the six-man OSS team that there were no incidents beyond the few rifle shots fired at Dr. Jarman as he descended in his 'chute. The Japanese knew that these half dozen men were backed by the might of a nation that could wipe an entire city out of existence with a single bomb. They also knew that thousands more Americans were poised at several hundred locations ready to strike at the first sign of resistance to the coming occupation.

The mission of the Peking OSS-Army team has remained shrouded in secrecy until now. Once the Japanese commander had confirmed to his troops that they were to offer no resistance and follow the orders of the Major and his men, the liberation of war prisoners began. The first to be liberated were the Allied prisoners located at the prison compound at Fengtai, four and a half miles southwest of Peking. Next were the prisoners in the military prison inside the walls of the city of Peking, including the Doolittle raiders. Their mission over, the OSS men faded away and regular Army troops began to occupy the city.

The four Doolittle raiders were located and released on the evening of August 20th. The Japanese guards had appeared at the cell doors of Nielsen, Hite and DeShazer and opened them wide. They led the three men to the wash room, gave them shaves and a bucket of hot water for washing—a rare treat—and then announced simply that the war was over. Barr, whose strange saga is covered in Chapter 10, was carried to the waiting room of the prison where he was reunited with his comrades.

The next several hours are hazy in the memories of these men today. The reality of freedom, although longed for so many months, was difficult to accept. But when they were taken to the Grand Hotel, an ancient edifice with a superabundance of servants, they felt that it would be only a short time until they would be returned home to their families. After four days of nourishing food and medical treatment, Dr. Fontaine G. Jarman, first man to jump to their rescue, authorized Nielsen, Hite and DeShazer, to proceed by air to Chungking via Kunming. "Barr will have to remain here a few days," Jarman told the three, "and catch up with you as soon as he gets his strength back."

The three lucky survivors said their goodbyes to Barr and left in a C-47 for Chungking. The press, clamoring for a press conference with the three men, were allowed

On the day of their release from the prison at Peiping, the survivors were given their old uniforms back and a haircut. Lt. George Barr was too sick to be evacuated, but the others were flown to Chungking and then returned to the States. (L to R) Lt. Robert L. Hite, Cpl. Jacob DeShazer, and Lt. Chase J. Nielsen. USAF Photo

to interview them after a short medical check and interrogation by intelligence officers. Weak and haggard, but smiling happily, they recounted their experiences in low, almost inaudible voices.

They spent that night in a house belonging to Prime Minister T. V. Soong which had been loaned to American Major General Ray T. Maddocks. The American air commander, Lt. General George Stratemeyer, gave them new AAF insignia and shoulder patches. A colonel dispensed iced bottled beer — a precious commodity in Chungking — and they ate toasted sandwiches. Colonel Robert L. Johnson gave each flyer three towels, three pairs of trousers, shaving equipment, toothbrushes and paste. Colonel Johnson's son, a flyer, had been taken prisoner in Italy but had escaped after twenty days in solitary confinement. Speaking to them like a father, he advised them to talk freely of their experiences and answer all questions, no matter how many times they might be asked the same thing. "That's the only way to forget," the colonel counseled.

After their release DeShazer, Nielsen and Hite (from left to right) answer questions at a press conference in Chungking on August 25, 1945. Office of War Information

Dr. William Rennie, of Buffalo, New York, commander of the station hospital who examined the three men, announced to the press that they were "in pretty good condition, all things considered." Their reflexes, he said, were slow but would improve.

Colonel Johnson told the press that some criticism had been leveled against the Army for parachuting the rescue teams to prisoner of war camps before the Japanese surrender was signed formally. This caused Chase Nielsen to remark, "If they had waited another month, we would have come out feet first."

The next day, the trio—still hollow-cheeked and weak—began their long trip home. They arrived in Washington on September 5th and checked in at Walter Reed Hospital, where they again met the press. George Barr, their buddy, was still in Peking.

9
. . . . .

TRIAL AND PUNISHMENT–
THE AMERICAN WAY

JUST SIX DAYS AFTER their release in Peking, Bob Hite, Chase Nielsen and Jake DeShazer had been interviewed at Chungking by Colonel Edward H. Young, Theater Judge Advocate for the U.S. Army. The main purpose of the interview was to determine the facts concerning their capture and imprisonment and identify all Japanese who may have been responsible for their mistreatment. The result was a nine-page report digesting the forty months of hell that the four survivors had endured. At its conclusion, Colonel Young stated in a letter to Washington, that he "would welcome any information or instruction from our National Office" concerning his next move in this case.

Plans for War Crime investigations upon cessation of hostilities had been laid many months before. As soon as the Japanese surrendered, teams of investigators were sent to the Chinese coastal areas where Allied prisoner of war camps were located. One team of two Judge Advocates, with interpreters and clerical personnel, was sent to the Hong Kong port area. Similar teams were sent to Shanghai, Mukden, and Peking. In addition, skilled interrogators interviewed all POW's who were evacuated by air through Chungking and Kunming. Hite, Nielsen and DeShazer, given top priority, were the first to pass through Chungking and be interrogated.

The three cheerful, though emaciated, Doolittle fliers gave a brief interview with the press after Colonel Young completed his interrogation and began their long but happy journey home. While the Allied world rejoiced in victory and the news of the liberation of hundreds of Americans from Japanese prisons, the U.S. Army investigation teams questioned them all in the search for names of Japanese who should be prosecuted. In a relatively short time, hundreds of Japanese were located who had been particularly cruel or had caused the death of prisoners either through neglect, stupidity, or design.

The investigation team assigned to Shanghai had special instructions to seek witnesses who could testify as to the treatment of the Doolittle raiders when they were in their city from August, 1942 until April, 1943. The team leader, an Army major and a Chinese officer, Lt. Peter Kim, had received a report from Caesar L. dos Remedios that, if needed, he would agree to testify in any trials that might be held for the Japanese. Remedios had promised the four Americans he had befriended when they left Shanghai for Nanking that if the Allies won the war and any American mission should ever come to Shanghai, he would tell them that the Doolittle fliers were alive and had been there.

Remedios was determined to keep his promise and did. His name was turned over to U.S. Army authorities and several weeks later he was contacted by Captain James S. Bailey, now assigned to the Doolittle flyer case as an investigator. Remedios told Bailey the incredible story from his viewpoint and proved that he knew whereof he spoke by turning over the pathetic personal belongings of Bill Farrow—his girl friend's photograph, traveler's cheques and other items from his billfold. Bailey was now convinced of the credibility of the man's testimony and took Remedios, his star witness, to the Military Prison outside the city. The former prison warden, Tatsuta, was no longer there but most of the guards were. "If looks could kill," Remedios said, "I would have been a dead one that day."

Bailey confronted the new warden and demanded the records of the Doolittle fliers through Remedios, who acted as his interpreter. The new warden shrugged and denied any knowledge of any American prisoners ever having been there. Lt. Tadahiro Hayama, a Japanese law officer and later one of the defense counsel for the defendants, interjected. "It is no use to deny the American's questions," he told the warden, "this man Remedios was also a prisoner when the Doolittle men were here. You will turn over the records."

Remedios proved to be of invaluable help to the investigation team. When the growing evidence was analyzed, it was decided that there was enough to bring charges against a number of Japanese. As a result, Colonel John H. Hendren and Major Robert T. Dwyer, both skilled lawyers, were assigned as prosecutors. Remedios was hired as an investigator and interpreter. His friendship for the men and his promise to bring those responsible for their cruel treatment to justice made the case a valid one. His diligence turned up the fact that the urns containing the ashes of Lieutenants Farrow and Hallmark and Sergeant Spatz were in the office of the International Funeral Parlor in Shanghai. Accompanied by Major Dwyer, Remedios went to the establishment but could not find the urns. But Remedios knew his information was correct. He discovered that the names on three boxes had been recently altered. Obviously, those responsible for or who had knowledge of the execution of the three men had

An investigating party at the execution site of three of Doolittle's Raiders in December 1945. Several Japanese were present as interpreters. The executions had taken place on October 15, 1942. PHOTO COURTESY CHASE J. NIELSEN

Three of the guards from Kiangwan Prison who witnessed the execution of Hallmark, Farrow, and Spatz pose at the execution site. (L to R) Minezaki, Yoneya and Mayama. PHOTO COURTESY CHASE J. NIELSEN

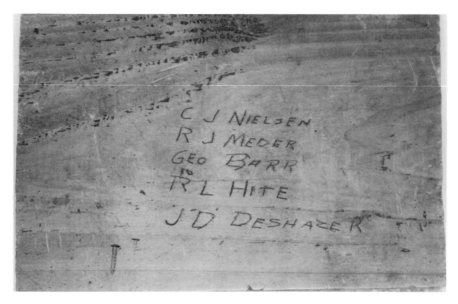

Chase Nielsen scratched his name and the names of his buddies in the floor of his cell at Kiangwan Prison, Shanghai. After the war, the board shown above was located by American authorities to prove that the Doolittle crew members had occupied that prison. The board is on permanent display at the Air Force Museum, Wright-Patterson AFB, Ohio. USAF Photo

Lt. Chase Nielsen (left) explains to War Crimes Trial prosecutors, Col. John H. Hendren and Capt. Robert T. Dwyer, why he inscribed the message on the floor board from his Kiangwan prison cell. Photo courtesy Chase J. Nielsen

hoped to cover up this gruesome evidence of their deaths. To Remedios, who knew of the Japanese penchant for precise record-keeping, the discovery was easy. Whoever had changed the names had not changed the birth dates on the tags. Hallmark's name had been changed to "J. Smith," Farrow had become "H. E. Gande," and Spatz was "E. L. Brister."

As the evidence mounted between August, 1945 and the following February, it was found that a long list of Japanese could be prosecuted for the unlawful treatment of the Doolittle fliers but because many were then deceased or accused of more serious war crimes, the number to be brought to trial in China was reduced to four: Lieutenant General Shigeru Sawada, commanding general of the Japanese Imperial Thirteenth Expeditionary Army; Captain Ryuhei Okada, a member of the mock court that tried the eight men; Lieutenant Yusei Wako, prosecutor during the mock trial, and Captain Sotojiro Tatsuta, the warden at Kiangwan Military Prison and official executioner of Hallmark, Farrow and Spatz. Major Itsuro Hata, the prosecutor at the mock trial and Lieutenant Colonel Toyarna Nakajo, the chief judge, had died. General Shunroku Hata, commanding general of all Japanese forces in China and Sawada's superior, and Lieutenant General Sadamu Shimomura, who succeeded Sawada as commander of the Thirteenth Army and actually signed the order of execution for the three airmen, were both held in Tokyo for prosecution by the International War Crimes commission. Their release for the Doolittle flyer trial was refused.

When the preliminary investigations were complete and the records had been unearthed in Japan, the order went out to American occupation units to locate and apprehend Sawada, Okada, Wako and Tatsuta. On February 27, 1946, the solemn quartet was arraigned before a Military Commission appointed by the Commanding General, United States Forces, China Theater. The commission promptly adjourned upon the motion of the defense counsel so that the defense could visit Japan to procure evidence, secure certain witnesses and prepare its case.

United States authorities were determined not only to bring to justice those accused of criminal acts against prisoners of war but also to provide a model court case so the Japanese could observe American justice in action. It had been long established in the history of the English-speaking world that appropriate safeguards under the laws of war should be accorded an accused war criminal which would include a fair and public trial, the right to counsel, and the right to make special pleas. Both the written and customary laws of war observed by the Allies were based on the premise that the fundamental rights of every individual must be protected and that captured personnel are entitled to an opportunity to make a defense at their trials and be protected against cruel and inhuman treatment and punishment.

The contrast between the trial the Japanese held for the Doolittle fliers and that of the four accused was marked. General Sawada and his three colleagues-in-crime were assigned qualified defense counsel by the United States Army. In addition, three Japanese attorneys were allowed at the request of the accused. The Japanese, on the other hand, had permitted the fliers no counsel or opportunity to make a defense and their own mock trial had lasted only a few minutes. In this, their own trial, the Japanese accused were allowed all the time they requested for the preparation of their defense. Their public trial lasted almost a month and the entire proceedings were interpreted in their own language and a verbatim record made. They were also provided free transportation to and from Japan for their witnesses and defense counsel. Thus, the United States afforded all the essential safeguards enumerated by the Articles of the Geneva Convention and otherwise recognized under the laws of war.

It was made clear to the four accused at their arraignment that the lawful maximum sentence that could be imposed for conviction of any war crime was death, although a lesser penalty was discretionary. They were now fighting for their own lives but they were made profoundly aware of one fact: their rights were going to be protected in the process and the trial was going to be as fair as the minds of free men could make it.

By March 18, after two postponements to allow the defense additional time for preparation, the trial began. The Military Commission trying the case consisted of Cols. Edwin R. McReynolds, John F. Gamber, Richard H. Wise and Joseph M. Murphy and Lt. Col. C. R. Berry. The Prosecutors were Lt. Col. John H. Hendren and Major Robert T. Dwyer. Defense Counsel was Lt. Col. Edmund J. Bodine and Capt. Charles R. Fellows, plus three Japanese lawyers, H. Komoshiro, T. Hayama and Shinji Somiya. Two court reporters, Miss Lillyan R. Moyle and Mr. Marshall H. Zeman were assigned and six interpreters, including Caesar L. dos Remedios, were sworn in to assure that there would be no misunderstandings in the interpretation of the proceedings.

At 9 A.M. on the morning of March 18, 1946, Colonel McReynolds called the court to order and the case of the United States versus Sawada, Tatsuta, Okada, and Wako began. The place of trial was the Ward Road Jail in Shanghai, which happened to be the place of temporary confinement for the accused. The first witness was Capt. Chase J. Nielsen, the only one of the four survivors who agreed to return to the Far East to face those responsible for the death, torture, and confinement of the two captured crews. Nielsen, who had sworn to himself that he would live to see this day, was now fit and trim. Tough and resilient in captivity, he was the ideal one of the four survivors to give testimony in their behalf. He spoke frankly and forcefully on behalf of the Prosecution. Under cross-examination by the defense, which was sometimes severe, Nielsen held up well although he unconsciously resented the fact that two American officers were defending the accused.

The major Japanese war criminals line up before being allowed to enter the courtroom at the Japanese War Ministry Building in Tokyo in June 1946. Directly in front of the guard is Admiral Osami Nagano, chief of the naval general staff 1940–1944. PHOTO COURTESY JOSEPH PRUETT

The entire prison staff of the Japanese military prison in Nanking, China pose for an official photograph. The surviving Doolittle Raiders were kept in solitary confinement here from 1943 to 1945. US ARMY PHOTO

View of walled prison at Shanghai where the surviving Raiders were kept for two years. Door to court-room where mock trial was held is at left. The prisoners were later transferred to Nanking and placed in small cells according to their heights. Lt. Robert J. Meder died at that prison of beri-beri and malnutrition. PHOTO COURTESY CHASE J. NIELSEN

A frightened Capt. Sotojiro Tatsuta, warden of Kiangwan Prison who gave the firing order in the execution of Farrow, Hallmark and Spatz, bows before Chase Nielsen at the Ward Road jail in Shanghai where the accused war criminals were held. Nielsen returned to China to testify against his captors in 1946. Tatsuta was sentenced to serve five years at hard labor; he died in 1962.

Photo courtesy Chase J. Nielsen

Under the careful questioning of Lt. Col. Hendren, Nielsen recounted his flight over Tokyo and his subsequent capture, torture, and imprisonment. Hendren particularly stressed questions about whether or not Nielsen's plane had bombed military targets and fired the plane's machine guns against civilians. Nielsen made it perfectly clear that General Doolittle's many briefings had stressed that they were only to bomb military objectives. The bombs from his plane were all dropped on the steel mill area, including the incendiary cluster. He also was firm in his testimony that none of the guns on his plane had been fired from the time they left the *Hornet* until they crashed.

The defense lawyers, Col. Bodine and Capt. Fellows, were alert and eager to defend the rights of the accused to the full extent of the law. They knew that not only the lives of the accused were at stake but also the entire American system of jurisprudence. While they were overruled in most of their objections, they never once missed a point of weakness in the prosecution's line of questioning.

Chase Nielsen testified intensively for two days. After Nielsen was dismissed from the stand, a 43-page question-and-answer deposition from George Barr was admitted in evidence. Barr had answered the questions of a security agent while near the end of his stay at Schick General Hospital in Clinton, Iowa, and had described his capture, torture, and treatment succinctly. The details agreed with Nielsen's testimony in most respects and was followed by a similar recounting of their experiences in a joint statement made by Bob Hite and Jacob DeShazer. They had been interrogated in Washington months before. The net result was the basis for the strong case of the prosecution against the accused.

The prosecution also introduced many additional witnesses to substantiate the stories of the four survivors, including such people as a Chinese named Teh Ling Chung, Russians named Alexander Hindrava and Alexander Sterelny who had all been in the cell with Dean Hallmark in the Bridge House Jail. Other witnesses were Japanese guards who had been present at the execution of Hallmark, Farrow and Spatz. An American medical officer, Col. George E. Armstrong, testified about the effects of beri-beri, especially as it could have caused the death of Bob Meder.

On March 26, the Commission went to the cemetery where the executions had been carried out. In addition, they visited the cell block at Kiangwan Prison where the men had been kept prisoners. The counsel for the prosecution and defense, the interpreters, an official court reporter, and Chase Nielsen made this visit, but the defendants declined the invitation.

The prosecution and defense completed their testimony in the case of the United States vs. Shigeru Sawada *et al.* on April 9, 1946. The court reconvened two days later to hear the summarizing arguments of the two sides. Not only the two American

The Honorable Mr. Justice Alan James Mansfield, associate prosecutor, introduces exhibits at the opening session of the trial of 28 accused Japanese war criminals before the International Military Tribunal for the Far East in Tokyo. The trial lasted more than two years and produced 49,000 pages of transcripts.
PHOTO COURTESY JOSEPH PRUETT

lawyers were permitted to present their arguments but also the Japanese defense lawyer, Kumashiro, who made an impassioned plea for the accused and thanked the court for "the impartial and earnest attitude of all the members of this Commission, prosecutors, interpreters, and the American defense counsel." He added that "it is deeply engraved in our hearts that this trial has not been motivated from some revengeful feeling towards their enemies, but that the United States wants to manifest through this trial her ideals to the world."

Capt. Fellows, in making the major portion of the defense's summation, recognized the importance of the case from an international point of view "because it is the first attempt by an American Military Commission to review the acts of a tribunal of another nation and to punish nationals of that nation who complied with those laws, rules and judicial decisions of that nation. This function is usually performed by an International Commission of selected jurists."

The case for the prosecution was summarized by Major Dwyer. He carefully reviewed the testimony of the prosecution witnesses and attacked the defense's case

View of the courtroom in the War Ministry Building in Tokyo where major war criminals were arraigned and tried, including Hideki Tojo, prime minister and war minister at the time of the raid on Pearl Harbor and most of the war. The justices on the left represent the eleven allied nations; defendants are on the right. PHOTO COURTESY JOSEPH PRUETT

for the accused on every point of substance. Slowly and with careful legal precision, the energetic Dwyer explained why the four accused were brought to trial and why "we think they should pay the supreme penalty of the law, each and every one." After two hours of steady argument, Dwyer said:

"I conclude by saying this: Four of these Doolittle fliers have paid the penalty with their lives, when, as a matter of fact, both on the evidence before the tribunal of August 28, 1942, and upon the evidence of this commission, they were entitled rightfully and objectively and by every standard to the status of prisoners of war, and at no time did they get it, and four of them died for it, and four others, if not for the power of the United Nations, would still be paying for it. The evil began when these men were placed before a tribunal, a tribunal of any kind; and secondly, once they were placed before it they had no more chance or opportunity of a fair and honest trial than I have with my right hand to stem the fall of Niagara's waters . . .

ADDRESS REPLY TO
HEADQUARTERS OF THE ARMY AIR FORCES
WAR DEPARTMENT
WASHINGTON, D. C.

WAR DEPARTMENT
HEADQUARTERS OF THE ARMY AIR FORCES
WASHINGTON

April 21, 1943.

TO ALL PERSONNEL OF THE ARMY AIR FORCES:

In violation of every rule of military procedure and of every concept of human decency, the Japanese have executed several of your brave comrades who took part in the <u>first</u> Tokyo raid. These men died as heroes. We must not rest - we must re-double our efforts - until the inhuman warlords who committed this crime have been utterly destroyed.

Remember those comrades when you get a Zero in your sights - have their sacrifice before you when you line up your bombsights on a Japanese base.

You have demonstrated that the Japanese cannot match you in aerial combat or in bombardment. Let your answer to their treatment of your comrades be the destruction of the Japanese Air Force, their lines of communication, and the production centers which offer them opportunity to continue such atrocities.

H. H. ARNOLD,
General, U. S. Army,
Commanding General, Army Air Forces.

3-8075, AF

When it was announced a year after the raid that the Japanese had executed several of the Doolittle Raiders, General Henry H. Arnold issued this notice which was distributed throughout the Army Air Forces. USAF PHOTO

"We have charged these men with the violations of the laws of custom and war. We have proven it by a wealth of evidence. We close by asking for the death penalty against all four of the accused."

The Commission adjourned on April 12th. Two days later the commission reconvened to present its conclusions:

"The offenses of each of the accused resulted largely from obedience to the laws and instructions of their Government and their military superiors. They exercised no initiative to any marked degree. The preponderance of evidence shows beyond reasonable doubt that other officers, including high governmental and military officials, were responsible for the enactment of the Ex Post Facto "Enemy Airmen's Law" and the issuance of special instructions as to how these American prisoners were to be treated, tried, sentenced and punished.

"The circumstances set forth above do not entirely absolve the accused from guilt. However, they do compel unusually strong mitigating considerations, applicable to each accused in various degrees."

The conclusions reached concerning the charges against each of the accused were reviewed and then the four sad-faced Japanese were asked to stand before the Commission to hear the findings. The courtroom fell silent as Colonel McReynolds, head of the Commission, announced the verdict of guilty against the defendants and then their sentences. To the surprise of the audience, including the accused, the sentences were relatively light. Although the maximum penalty could have been death, the Commission believed the mitigating circumstances justified much lighter sentences. Sawada, Okada and Tatsuta were each sentenced to five years confinement at hard labor. Wako, the lawyer, received a nine-year sentence, presumably because he was a lawyer and knew that the "Enemy Airmen's Act" had been enacted after the Tokyo Raid, specifically to the detriment of the eight fliers.

The four prisoners were led away to separate cells at the Ward Road Jail in Shanghai to await the results of a review of their trial. In August, the legal advisors to Gen. Albert C. Wedemeyer, commander of the American forces in China, deemed the charges and the trial adequate and proper but disagreed with the leniency shown by the court in awarding such light sentences when the maximum penalty could have been death. Col. Edward H. Young, Wedemeyer's staff judge advocate, wrote in his review of the case that the trial of the four was fair and impartial and the sentences legal. However, he pointed out that the Commission "by awarding such extremely lenient and inadequate penalties committed a serious error of judgment." He added that "It is clear that when they found the accused guilty of the capital offenses of mistreatment and murder under the laws of war, the penalties should have been commensurate with

The ashes of Lts. Meder, Hallmark and Farrow were brought to the United States in 1946 and interred in the Arlington National Cemetery. Sgt. Spatz's ashes are interred in the National Cemetery in Hawaii. PHOTOS BY HAROLD WISE

the findings. On the other hand, as the principal issues of the very case it was adjudging involved the illegal performance of judicial functions under the laws of war by the accused, and with few recorded precedents available, the Commission membership no doubt was particularly conscious of its own obligations in this regard. Accordingly, it is then pertinent to note that if an error of judgment was made, then contrary to the Japanese idea of justice and humanity, the Commission favored the accused with all the benefits thereof."

No sentence can be increased by a reviewing authority under the American concept of justice so Col. Young recommended that the sentences of the accused stand and Gen. Wedemeyer agreed. A short time later, the four prisoners were transferred to Sugamo Prison in Tokyo where many other Japanese were to serve their sentences meted out at the International War Crimes Trials.

Public reaction in the United States when the sentences were announced was immediate. Parents and relatives of the four men who had died at the hands of these men wrote emotion-filled indignant letters to President Truman and members of Congress. One California woman wrote that "this is the most outrageous miscarriage of justice yet." She added that "I cannot express words to express my indignation. Hanging is too good for the Japs who murdered these helpless young airmen. President Roosevelt would never have permitted such a travesty to happen."

The 3,000 members of the Tulsa, Oklahoma, American Legion Post No. 577 wrote to General Dwight D. Eisenhower, then Army Chief of Staff, "protesting the absurd and ridiculously inadequate sentences" and urged "that new trials be held, presided over by competent officials; and that the officials who presided over the trial . . . be relieved of further duty with war crime trials."

All letters of protest were promptly and courteously answered. Most replies noted that the International Prosecution Staff had served an indictment on twenty-eight of the principal government and military leaders of Japan for war crimes "including such matters as the issuance of orders for the 'trial' and execution of the Doolittle fliers." The replies also noted that it was hoped that those responsible for issuing the orders "will be convicted for their crimes . . . and receive a just punishment."

The protests were academic. A fair trial had been held in which the accused had been assured of their rights every step of the way. The accused were judged on the basis of the evidence for and against them. The extenuating and mitigating circumstances were duly noted and sentences passed. The entire case was reviewed with dispassion and the sentences approved.

In their grief, the families of Hallmark, Farrow, Spatz and Meder can be forgiven for their bitterness. Their sons and brothers had fought to preserve the American way of life based on a system of law which recognized the dignity and the rights of all men. These four brave, young men had paid the ultimate price to help preserve that system.

Twenty years after the trial of the four Japanese, the author attempted to learn whether or not they had served their full sentences. Three of the four (Sawada, Okado and Tatsuta) had all been released from Sugamo Prison on January 9, 1950, after having served a term of four years and three months. Tatsuta died in September, 1962. Okado became an instructor at Rittsho University in Tokyo while General Sawada, almost blind, was never able to work again. None of these three men was bitter after their release and they felt that they had been justly tried. All had fully expected the death sentence and were grateful that their lives were spared.

Yusei Wako, the law officer at the mock trial, had received the longest sentence (nine years). After the Shanghai trial he was tried on other charges emanating from the war and received an additional sentence of imprisonment at hard labor for life. However, he was released in December, 1958 and resumed his law practice in the firm of his father. He is extremely bitter at the thirteen years of his life that were wasted behind bars and has no remorse for his part in the deaths of Hallmark, Farrow, and Spatz. All attempts to interview him were unsuccessful until April, 1965 when he reluctantly granted a telephone interview. Asked about the additional sentence he served, he flew into a rage and refused to discuss it. His health rapidly deteriorating, he became less and less active in his law practice.

It is probable that all four of these men are now deceased. Wako, born in 1909, was the youngest of the accused. Okada was past sixty and Sawada was approaching eighty in the mid-1960s; both were in ill health at that time. If they have died, their passing was not noted in the United States or Japan.

The Japanese people will be forever guilty of the deaths of the four Doolittle raiders and the "special" treatment of the four who came home. The author, in an attempt to locate and question Sawada, Okado, and Wako, contacted Susumu Nishiura, chief of the War History Office of the Japanese Self Defense Agency. His answers were polite and prompt. However, inside the material he sent was an unsigned paper entitled "Indiscriminate Bombing is Unlawful in International Law" which might well represent the Japanese conscience. Apparently in the hope that the author would use it as a sort of last word, it seeks to show that the Japanese had a perfect right to execute three of the Americans and imprison the others for life. The basis for this rationalization is that "the defendants' counsel has produced many undeniable and powerful proofs that civilians, schools, etc. which had no connection with military objectives were machine-gunned in the low flight of from 200 to 300 meters, according to which it is absolutely undeniable in view of the weight of the evidences that the Doolittle fliers made indiscriminate air-raiding attack, disregarding International Law."

It seems strangely ironic that in all the pleadings for the defense to show that the Doolittle planes bombed and strafed nonmilitary targets in violation of the laws of war, not once is the sneak attack on Pearl Harbor ever mentioned. The "day of infamy" has been quickly forgotten by the Japanese while the surprise raid by sixteen Mitchell bombers led by the incomparable Jimmy Doolittle still lingers in the minds of those who sought to rule the world. Perhaps the Japanese will never forget the Doolittle raid. After all, it was this single air mission, in which all planes were lost to the Allied cause, that marked the beginning of the end of Japanese militarism and the shattering of their dreams of empire.

10

THE LAST TO RETURN

GEORGE BARR WAS, by far, the sickest of the four survivors on their liberation day. He could not have survived another week of imprisonment and he knew it. In the few conscious moments he had during the last few days in the Peking Prison, the thought kept going through his mind that his struggle for life would soon be over. Like Meder, who had died quietly in his cell more than twenty-one months before, Barr was sure he was going to die in the same way.

On the evening of August 9, the day that the second atomic bomb was dropped on Nagasaki, George Barr went to sleep as soon as the light faded in his cell. Now just a skeleton, he did not regain consciousness for several days. When he did, he found himself in a heap on the floor of a different cell. He tried to untangle his arms and legs but the effort exhausted him. He stared at the ceiling and walls and fought through the fog of unconsciousness to reason again. Was he dead yet? If not, why was he in another cell? How did he get there? Was he even in the same jail? Where were the other fellows?

The questions kept repeating themselves over and over and remained unanswered. Barr tried to roll over and stand up but his legs wouldn't support his body. With nothing to hold onto in the bare cell he couldn't even claw his way to a half upright position. A sudden overwhelming urge to move his bowels caused him to search out the *benjo*—if there was one. He finally found it after what seemed like an hour of searching and dragged himself inch by inch toward it. For the next eleven days he lived in a dream world of semiconsciousness and delirium. The food bowls pushed through the hole in the cell door went untouched. Starved as he was, he had lost all interest in food. Even if he had wanted it he could not have reached it.

The Japanese guards did not open the cell door to check on Barr's condition. A hand would reach in for the untouched bowl but not once did a guard think it curious that a prisoner did not eat his pitiful allowance of fish, soup and rice.

As the hours of nothingness dragged on highlighted only by occasional moments of lucidity, Barr wondered what it took to make a man die. He thought he was already dead at times, yet he was frightened at the loneliness of it. Where was the serene happiness that death was supposed to bring to the soul? Could it be that his life after death was to continue to be the same stench and filth that he had known for over three years? Many times he tried to cry out his anguish but no sound would come.

It was the evening of August 20th that the stillness of unconsciousness was broken by the sudden opening of the cell door. The rasping creak of the door hinge and the gush of light startled Barr's benumbed brain and blinded him. He felt an over-whelming relief that death had finally come. Through the haze of blinding light, he saw the impassive face of a Japanese guard and felt himself being picked up like a child and carried down the corridor to a small room at the end of the cell block where he was laid out on a bench like a store dummy. His feet and legs were stretched out flat and his hands positioned across his stomach.

"So this is what it's like to die" Barr thought. "I'm still conscious, yet I'm not." He rather enjoyed the detachment he felt and the smell of freedom that slowly seeped into his nostrils. Suddenly out of the mixture came a familiar voice. It was Chase Nielsen's.

"Hi, George. How do you feel?"

Barr couldn't answer. Death was good after all. Death meant that you would join your buddies. Another voice came through. It was Bob Hite with his familiar western drawl. Or was it Hite? It had been so long since he had heard him speak.

"Come on, George, wake up! It's all over now. The war's over, George. We're free!"

The word "free" was like a hypodermic. Barr opened his eyes and focused guardedly on the scrawny, unshaven but still familiar faces of Nielsen, Hite, and DeShazer. They were smiling.

"I couldn't believe it was true," Barr recalled. "I *knew* I was dead now but I didn't care. If death meant that I could be with my three buddies, I was as happy as they were."

The events of the next few hours are still hazy to the tall redhaired Barr. He was quickly loaded into the back end of a truck and moved by solicitous Japanese guards to the Grand Hotel des Wagon Lits which had been hurriedly turned into a hospital in the center of the teeming city of Peking. Two Englishmen just released from a Japanese internment camp in another part of the city picked Barr up and carried him from the truck to a small room on the fifth floor of the hotel. Nielsen, Hite and DeShazer, all able to walk, were guided to an adjoining room. An English physician, Dr. Stephen D. Sturton, immediately took charge. He had been released only hours before from the nearby Fengtai prison compound along with several hundred other civilian internees of many nationalities. A Dutchman, Karel F. Mulder, assistant to Dr. Sturton, tells what he recalls of that eventful day:

"They all looked bad to me when they arrived at the Grand Hotel and George Barr was barely conscious when he arrived by stretcher. I assisted one of them, I forget whom, up the stairs to the fifth floor (the elevators were not running) although I did not have much strength. We were both so weak after climbing each flight of steps we sat down to rest. In the end we made it and I got him to bed.

"The next day medical supplies were dropped by U.S. planes which included blood plasma. We immediately gave blood to Barr and also one or two of the other Doolittle fliers. These men were by far the weakest prisoners we had seen since our own release and it was obvious that they had not received any medical treatment for a long time. When I realized that they had been in prison for forty months, I was amazed that there was any spark of life left."

Hite, Nielsen, and DeShazer were assigned one room while Barr was put in an adjoining room alone and given an injection which immediately put him to sleep. Meanwhile, the other three prisoners in the next room were beside themselves with their newly found freedom. They talked incessantly about their experiences with other Americans, Canadians, and British who had just been released and ate any kind of food they could lay their hands on and would stay down in their shrunken stomachs.

Barr awoke late the next morning with a strange feeling of elation he hadn't known since the day of the raid over three years before. His eyes cleared gradually and he could make out the various objects in the room. He delighted in the sight of familiar objects he had not seen for a long time, such as a dresser, chairs, glass windows without bars and a bed. And how good the bed felt! The happiness swelled within him but was it real or had he finally arrived in the Valhalla of all good airmen?

His eyes came to rest on a contraption beside him. It was a metal stand which held an upended bottle. There was a rubber tube attached to the bottle through which thick clear fluid was dripping slowly. His eyes followed the tube downward and he was surprised to see that it ended in his arm. The sight frightened him and he called out. A Chinese orderly appeared and assured him in halting English that the fluid was blood plasma, a life-saving fluid that had been developed during the war. "It will give you strength," he was told, "and you will soon be well again."

George Barr felt better then but a seed of suspicion had been planted which was to haunt him for many months to come. He had never heard of blood plasma and the unexpected appearance of an Oriental to his call surprised him. He suddenly had an overwhelming longing for the companionship of his three prison-mates and asked to be moved in with them. Dr. Sturton, in conference with Lt. (Dr.) Fontaine G. Jarman, the Air Force medic who had jumped with the OSS liberation team, agreed that it would speed George's recovery and he was moved into the next room immediately.

"That move of my bed those few feet helped to make that day one of the happiest of my life," he recalled. "My tongue fell all over itself trying to form words and sentences to go with the happy thoughts racing through my mind. I tried to express my feelings of complete joy but words were hard to come by after not having held a conversation with anyone for so many months. I knew I was babbling like a crazy man but I didn't care. I was free; I was with my buddies; I was soon going home."

The next three days were filled with the sounds and smells of freedom as the four Doolittle fliers exchanged stories of their imprisonment with British, Dutch, French, and Canadian ex-prisoners. Two Russian pilots, Lts. I. L. Pelty and M. K. Kiselev, who had been shot down in the nine-days' war between Russia and Japan, shared their common elation. The four Americans chain-smoked American cigarettes and stuffed themselves with K-rations, which they had never seen before. The packaged tidbits, which thousands of ex-GI's learned to loathe during the war, tasted as good as Crackerjack to these four starved men and they enjoyed every bite. Each package was American through and through and the thought made their spirits soar.

But forty months of starvation and being reduced to the level of animals could not be forgotten overnight. Each of them, without mentioning it to the others, stuffed extra packets of crackers, jelly, candy and cigarettes they could not consume in and under their beds. For all they knew, the rumors that the war was over might be false and they might be thrown back into their cells. They each decided that they wouldn't take any chances that Peking was only enjoying a temporary respite from war and they would soon be back in prison.

The suspicions that lurked in the subconscious of all the men loomed strongest in Barr's. For three days, he made no mention of it but without warning, he received a shock he was not mentally ready to take. Word had been received by the OSS team that the Doolittle raiders were to receive the highest travel priority and that a plane was coming to evacuate Bob Hite, Chase Nielsen and Jake DeShazer on the morning of the 24th. Drs. Jarman and Sturton and a Chinese, Dr. Wu, concurred that George Barr was too weak to be moved and would have to wait until he was stronger. George had no inkling that he would not go with his buddies and when they crowded around his bed to say goodbye, it was a surprise he was unprepared to meet. Before he realized it they were gone.

Sensing that Barr was greatly disturbed, the medics gave him an injection to make him rest. Meanwhile, twenty-six ex-prisoners — British, Canadian and American — were whisked to the airport and escorted aboard a converted B-24 Liberator. They were flown to Hsian and next day to Chungking. After a quick medical check-up and interrogation by intelligence officers, they were permitted to give a short press conference and then departed the same day for the United States. While they flew home to their loved ones, the radio waves of the world buzzed with the news that four of the eight missing Doolittle raiders had been found. The brief interview the three of them had given the press in Chungking made front page news around the world. Their story of torture and beatings caused renewed interest in the raid that had made air history forty months before. Writers speculated that the other four had been executed as the Japanese had intimated in late 1942 since there was no news of their whereabouts.

When George Barr awoke from his drugged sleep on the morning of August 25, he noticed the empty beds in his room but forgot that his three buddies had left. "Where did they go?" he shouted to someone in a bed nearby.

"Oh, they were all taken out and flown home yesterday," he was told by a Canadian roommate. "They said you were too sick to be moved and would go home later. Don't you remember saying goodbye to them yesterday?"

The Canadian's words and his follow-up question were like stab wounds to Barr. True, he was sick and weak but how could he be so ill he couldn't be moved by air to an American hospital elsewhere in China? Why had he forgotten that he had said goodbye? From the recesses of his mind the suspicion returned that he had felt the morning he awoke with the blood plasma in his arm. Had he dreamed all those things that he thought had happened in the four rapturous days just passed?

In the bed next to him, the medics had moved Mark King, a former English policeman who had served on the Shanghai Police Force during the occupation until the Japanese thought it was unsafe to allow this practice to continue. King had been confined in Fengtai but, like the others interned with him, had suffered only minor indignities and hardships compared to the prisoners in the military prison. Recognizing Barr's shock at being left behind, King tried to cheer him up. He encouraged Barr to write letters home and arranged to have a radio and a phonograph brought in. This helped the gaunt red-haired Barr's morale tremendously and when the novelty of hearing Kate Smith records and the good news of the plans for the Japanese surrender ceremony then being planned wore off, King told stories about his days as a Shanghai policeman. The tales of opium den raids, murders and brothel operations kept Barr's mind occupied and he appreciated King's efforts.

Under the frequent ministrations of Drs. Jarman, Sturton and Wu, Barr gained strength quickly. About a week after Hite, Neilsen and DeShazer had left, Barr was able to walk around with the aid of a cane. He was persuaded to write more letters, which he did with great difficulty. He visited with other men who were recuperating and awaiting evacuation and chatted amiably. In between walks he lay listening to the pre-war phonograph records and the English news broadcasts. The old doubts still lingered, however, especially when he realized that he was the only American ex-prisoner left in Peking.

As his stomach began to accept more food, he ate five or six times a day. One day he over-indulged and ate too many of the highly concentrated chocolate bars from one of the food packets. The stomach discomfort that followed reminded him of the old familiar dysentery he had had so long ago. He couldn't sleep that night and asked for a sleeping pill.

The combination of the upset stomach, the sleeping pill, his still-weakened condition, and the slowly gnawing suspicion erupted into a harrowing nightmare by dawn. He dreamed he was back in the strait jacket again gasping for air. He felt the stinging slaps on his head with the heavy belt and the jarring rifle butt in his ribs. Screaming at the top of his lungs in his imagined agony, he woke himself up.

Alone in the semi-darkness, George clutched the sides of his bed. His eyes bulged with fear and perspiration oozed from every pore. His mind froze into a curious fixation that was to remain with him for many months. He describes the obsession that gripped him:

"As I lay there panting in the half light, I told myself that I was the victim of a cruel hoax — that all that was happening was just one more Japanese torture. And the more I thought about it, the more pieces I could make to fit into my pattern of rationalization. Since nothing else had worked — the starvation, the tortures, the beatings, the solitary confinement — I figured they were now going to try the 'nice guy' approach to break me.

"I never felt more alone than at that moment, even when I was in solitary. I remembered then that all the other Americans had vanished from Peking. In spite of all I had been told about the war being over, Japanese soldiers still roamed the streets in uniform; Japanese police still directed traffic. The war was supposed to be over, yet I could hear guns in the distance.* Everyone had said I was free but I couldn't go anywhere.

"I then began to think about the medical treatment I had been given. That so-called blood plasma, could it have been doped? I had never heard of plasma before. The dextrose solution that I had watched drip into my body by the hour, could it have been some sort of truth serum? And why had most of the attendants been Chinese? Or were they Japanese? I could never tell them apart. Where were the American doctors and medical corpsmen? What had they done with my buddies? Why had I been singled out to remain behind in China if the war was really over?

"What might have been the fantasy of a nightmare now turned into fact as far as I was concerned. The next morning I eyed the foreigners around me with great distrust. I was now positive that the Japanese had devised a new method of torture

---

*By this time Chinese Nationalists were engaging Chinese Communist troops on the outskirts of Peking.

as part of my 'special treatment.' I was supposed to think that I was free yet my every move was being watched. I suspected that I was surrounded by Japanese spies who called themselves 'friends' to gain my confidence. From that moment on, I would pretend to go along with them but I was determined inwardly to resist this new kind of enemy torment with all the will power I had left."

Barr's screams had awakened the Canadian, Mark King, in the next bed. "What's the matter, Old Chap?" King called cheerily. "Have a bad dream?"

Barr snapped his head around and stared at his questioner. To Barr, King's eyes had suddenly developed a definite Oriental slant and his manner seemed overly solicitous. He was one of them, Barr thought, and refused to answer the question.

King was puzzled by this change in Barr's demeanor and kept on trying to cheer him up in spite of the silent rebuff. But the more King tried, the more Barr's suspicions were confirmed. King relayed his concern that Barr was becoming mentally disoriented to the medics and their increased attention gave still more credence to Barr's doubts and fears.

On September 12th, Barr was placed on a stretcher, taken to the airport and flown to Kunming where he was assigned to Ward 15 of the 172nd General Hospital. A letter had been forwarded ahead stating that Barr had been emotionally unstable, had paranoid tendencies and had been subject to amnesia after what had seemed to be a normal recovery from the effects of his solitary confinement and malnutrition.

"They were right in diagnosing my symptoms," Barr said, "but they didn't know that I had what I honestly believed were perfectly logical reasons for acting the way I did. To their way of thinking, I had turned into a mental patient and could not be responsible for what I said or did. When they took me off the airplane at Kunming and put me in a bare room by myself, I was *positive* then that everyone had been brainwashed by the Japanese somehow and were under their control. The faces and voices I had come to know in Peking had now changed. Although everyone seemed properly solicitous as they 'processed' me in, no one smiled. The young medics treated me as if I were either a child or a doddering old man.

"Every few minutes after my arrival, a face would appear, look at me and disappear. Then another face would come. No one would say anything—just take my pulse or my temperature and leave. It was almost as if they thought I was unconscious. When I tried to talk to them I got short, clinical answers in return. I had the feeling that it was like the hundreds of days and nights when the Japanese guards peered into our cells on their rounds. The only difference was that my door was open now and there were no bars on the windows.

"Looking back on it now, the medics were absolutely right when they said I was emotionally unstable. I cried at this reversal of my so-called freedom. They said I was paranoid because of my delusions of persecution but what else could I be when there was no one to trust and confide with. There wasn't a friendly, familiar voice or face around and after forty months in a cell I thought I was back in one now. I didn't have amnesia but I can see how they thought I did when I felt that I would rather say nothing than incriminate myself in some way by my answers to their overly solicitous questions."

To the medical personnel in the hospital, Barr was just another disturbed patient who would be kept there until he recovered sufficiently to be returned to the States. The following excerpts from the official "Nurse's Notes" graphically shows their observations as he wavered between reality and abnormalcy:

15 September 1945

1500 Admitted per ambulance to Wd 15. Seems to be rather dazed. Ate very small amt. of food.
1930 Collapsed. Extremely weak. Lifted into bed clinging to jacket. Restless and suspicious. Refused fluids. States they are doped. Refuses thermometer.
2000 Seen by major. Appears to understand more clearly. Took medicine after persuasion. Drank eggnog.
2230 Complained of severe pains in left knee and ankle.
2330 Has not slept. Restless. Given eggnog.
2400 States leg pain less severe and that he wishes to talk to someone. Talked quietly for one hour. Dwelled on past experiences and tortures. Continuously attempts to describe the effects of opium. Cheerful and cooperative.

Barr rested quietly the rest of that night and ate a nearly normal breakfast. Medication to ease abdominal and leg pains and vitamin shots were administered and he seemed to relax all the next day. However, at 6:45 P.M. as he was dozing fitfully, he fell out of the high hospital bed. The shock of the fall unnerved him and, as the Nurses Report noted, became "irrational" and "uncooperative." He was given a shot to quiet him and slept until after midnight. Another shot was then given. The Nurses' Report cryptically stated:

Awoke suddenly at 2 A.M. jumped out of bed screaming. Put into bed. Restrained by three men. Gritted teeth and uttered animal-like sounds with occasional threats to his "torturers." Sodium amytol—7 grains. Seen by M.O.D.

Sleeping. Pulse very weak. Transferred to Ward 13 at 2:30 A.M.

Ward 13 was the psychiatric ward and when Barr awoke the next morning, he knew right away that he was not in the same room he had occupied when he went to sleep the evening before. Now the floor and walls were padded; the only other furniture in the room besides the bed he lay in was a single chair. Light streamed through a barred window cut high in one wall. Barr recalls his reactions as his mind cleared:

"All my past suspicions and doubts were now confirmed. The barren room, the bars, the occasional face at a slot in the locked door, the solitary confinement spelled prison as far as I was concerned. I lay there a long time thinking things over and decided that I would pretend to go along with anything my captors were trying to make me do—but I would never give up trying to escape when the chance appeared. If they wanted stories from me, I would give them stories. If they wanted to experiment with my body, I certainly didn't have the strength to stop them. If they were trying to punish me for something, I would try to learn what it was and prevent any recurrence. But I would prepare myself to escape at the first opportunity. No one, I told myself, would *ever* brainwash me as they had apparently done to all the white people I had met so far since those stinking days in the Peking prison."

The medical reports for the next two weeks reflect Barr's progress toward regaining physical health and also his continuing mental wrestling with reality. Words like "apprehensive," "restless," "agitated," and "disturbed" appeared frequently as the Army medical personnel recorded his case dispassionately. It was this irrational behavior that kept their patient in the padded cell as far as they were concerned. From Barr's point of view, it was being kept in the cell that further confirmed the belief that he was still a prisoner in the hands of the enemy.

The news of Barr's case spread rapidly through the hospital. All of the released prisoners were newsworthy because of what they had been through but this tall, gaunt, red-haired lieutenant was a special case. In his moments of calm, occasioned by the tranquilizing drugs he was given, he talked of his life before the war, his flying training and the raid on Nagoya. The enlisted medics, accustomed to dealing with mental patients, did not believe he was actually one of the Doolittle crew members. The general public had remembered the raid, of course, but very few outside the families of the Doolittle Raiders themselves knew what had happened to the individuals concerned or could recall their names. When Hite, Nielsen and DeShazer had been interviewed, some of the newspapers had erroneously reported that all four of the surviving prisoners taken after the Tokyo Raid had been flown back to the States. With no records of any kind to substantiate his identity, the evidence of mental disturbance and the confusion of the end of the war with demobilization in full swing, George Barr was just another patient in an overcrowded overseas hospital. His adjustment was a problem for a psychiatrist. If he showed no progress, he would be one of those cases who would be taken home to the States in a strait jacket.

In spite of the misunderstanding and seeming apathy toward his case, however, one medical officer was greatly concerned about this patient. He was Dr. (Capt.) Werner Tuteur who took a special interest in Barr because he believed the stories about the tortures he had suffered and understood the rationalizing that Barr's confused mind was going through. Barr slowly began to trust the young, sympathetic Westerner, and responded more and more to Tuteur's patient questioning.

"If I'm not a prisoner," Barr asked him suddenly one morning, "why are there bars on the window and door?"

The bars were promptly removed.

"If I'm not a prisoner," he asked again, "why can't I leave my room?"

Tuteur opened the door and quietly told Barr that he could go outside if he wanted to.

"If you say there's nothing wrong with me," Barr countered, then why can't I be put in the ward with the other fellows?"

Tuteur immediately assigned him a bed in the large open bay with about ten other psychiatric patients. The highly charged diet was changed and Barr tasted his first ice cream and cookies. He was issued a uniform and saw his first movie. The effect on Barr's mental state was immediately evident. The Nurse's Notes for the next several days show the effect of the change in treatment on him:

> 18 Sept 45 Still apprehensive but less confused this A.M. Interviewed by Capt Tuteur. Very sociable and talkative. Spoke of his home life freely. Ate large lunch. No signs of anxiety or excitability.

> 19 Sept 45 Patient does not appear to be apprehensive nor confused this morning. Laughing and talking—seems quite happy. Appetite very good—out in wheel chair for short period this afternoon.

> 21 Sept 45 Very pleasant and talkative. Enjoyed lunch of Stateside cookies. Thinks we are doing too much for him.

> 23 Sept 45 Cheerful and friendly this A.M. Seems much less confused.

In spite of his apparent progress toward mental readjustment, Barr had a sudden relapse on September 24th. At 2 P.M., the ward nurse reported that he "became very apprehensive—asked why we didn't kill him right away." The reports for the next few days show similar regressions as the suspicions fostered by forty months of imprisonment lurked in the corners of his still-confused mind.

A medical corpsman, Cpl. Ernest W. Manley, of Whitesboro, New York, also took a special interest in Barr. The young medic was assigned to "special" the tall red-head which meant staying with him all day, taking him outside in a wheelchair, and helping him to regain his strength and normal mental outlook by having him meet nurses, enlisted personnel and other patients. Besides Dr. Tuteur, Barr now had another friend and this meant a lot to the Doolittle raider who had been orphaned in his childhood and had grown up in a foster home.

While the mental lapses continued, they became less frequent. Since Manley had earned enough points to return to the States, he was told that as soon as Barr could be moved by air, the two of them would be given orders to return home, with Manley acting as medical attendant. Both men were happy about the prospect and it hastened Barr's recovery, although he had a temporary setback as a result of a bad sunburn which he thought might be a new form of Japanese torture.

On October 1st, a board of medical officers met and recommended Barr's evacuation to a General Hospital in the Zone of Interior by ship "since his course of treatment will take considerable time." As far as the record was concerned, "Case No. 269" was to be closed as soon as the patient departed.

Both Barr and Manley excitedly "sweated out" the rumors that orders were being issued which would enable them to get transportation by hospital ship to the States from Calcutta. On October 9, Manley was ordered to gather up his and Barr's belongings and the two of them were to proceed to the Kunming airport. When they arrived, Manley checked in at the base operations passenger counter and was told to take his patient to a waiting C-47 transport. The two men started across the wide aircraft parking ramp with Manley supporting Barr by the arm. Barr looked beyond the plane toward the mountains in the distance and felt an overwhelming sense of emancipation and freedom. He realized that this was the first time that he had a visual horizon without restriction in over three years. The wide open space of the aidrome, the clear air, the blue sky and the lack of physical restraint were almost too good to be true.

Like a gun shot, a blaze of terror shot through Barr's mind. Here he was free at last! No one could stop him now! This was the moment he had dreamed of for so very, very long. From the depths of his soul the desire to flee from his "captors" sought release. With a strength born of desperation, he bolted away from Manley and started to run across the airstrip, his wide eyes fixed on the mountains many miles away. Now nothing and nobody could stop him. The Japanese with all their fiendish tortures, had not imagined that he could run but he would show them. He was free, free, free at last!

Out of nowhere, a blow felled Barr like a log and he dropped to the ramp in an unconscious heap. When he regained his senses, he was on a stretcher in flight aboard a C-47. His arms were encased in a strait jacket and he was lying under a restraining sheet. Ernie Manley was gone. There were other men in stretchers stacked three deep along the center aisle. Several officer passengers were in the rear of the plane napping. A medical attendant came down the aisle checking the patients and Barr asked him where he was. The medic checked the restraining sheet and smiled at the question but did not answer. The war-weary C-47 groaned on hour after hour and finally, after several stops for gas, arrived at Calcutta, India.

Barr's questions about his status, his condition or where he was going were never answered. He was off-loaded at Calcutta and whisked to a hospital where he was taken out of the strait jacket and put in an open ward. He complained of a bad toothache and a dentist promptly extracted it. That night, recovering from the effects of the novocaine, he had another awesome nightmare and was placed in a padded room again. The old suspicion returned and, again, the pieces fitted together perfectly. He was really still a prisoner. He had been flown to someplace they said was Calcutta but what evidence did he have that he was even in India? Why had they put him in restraint for the flight it he weren't still at the mercy of the fiendish Japanese? Where were Ernie and Dr. Tuteur, the only men he could trust? It was just like the Japanese to build up his confidence then shatter it. Again, there were new faces, new surroundings, new smells and, again, no one to confide with or answer questions. Everyone he saw looked to him as if they were hypnotized. When would this farce stop? Why were they doing all this?

"I decided then and there," Barr said, "that I would foil their plot, whatever it might be, by not weakening no matter what. I would be a good boy if that was what they wanted and the next time I got the chance to escape, I would make sure the odds against getting away were a lot better before I made a break for it."

Barr's pretense at being "normal" worked. He talked freely with the medical attendants and was allowed to walk around the ward without restraint. After three days, he was told that he would be going back to the States with three other officers who had earned enough points to separate from the service. Barr didn't know what "points" meant but decided it was just another gimmick in an ingenious Japanese scheme to break him. On October 7th, orders were issued authorizing Lt. Cols. Harold L. Decker, Junior Rich, and Clinton C. Millett to proceed "without delay by first available aircraft to San Francisco, California as attendants to 2d Lt. George Barr . . . for delivery of patient to nearest General Hospital in Zone of Interior." Decker was an infantry officer but the other two were physicians. Their responsibility was to watch Barr around the clock and make sure he didn't harm himself while they traveled. Their reward was the privilege of traveling to the States on his travel priority.

The four men boarded a C-47. Barr was unrestrained but carefully watched as the plane took off. As the plane turned eastward, Barr asked his escorts, "Where are we going?"

"To Kunming," one of them answered without elaborating.

This answer was just another thread to be woven into the cloth of chicanery. Barr was a navigator and knew his geography. The shortest way to the States from China by air would be eastward across the Pacific—the direction from which the Raiders had come in 1942. Calcutta was in the opposite direction but once there, why had they retraced their steps back to Kunming?

Barr fell silent as the ancient C-47 droned on mile after mile over the treacherous mountains making up the "Hump." He eyed his three escorts suspiciously and wondered why so many Americans had been taken in by the Japanese. Had the Orientals discovered some drug that had enabled them to subjugate their captives? Maybe that's why their skin was so yellow in spite of the fact that they had said it was from atabrin. If these three men wearing the silver leaves of U.S. Army lieutenant colonels were really Americans, why was there a Japanese samurai sword sticking out of each of their duffel bags? Each answer that he supplied himself was just another link in the incredible chain of circumstances in the strange saga of George Barr.

Barr never found out why he had to return to Kunming except to pick up another officer who had somehow arranged to go home as an escort officer so he, too, could travel on the Barr priority . Shortly after arrival in Kunming, the five men boarded a C-54 and flew to Manila, Guam, and Johnson Island, where Barr was put in a tin shed while the plane was being gassed. The confusion in Barr's mind deepened as the lumbering transport took off again and droned on and on. With nothing to look at outside the plane and faces he didn't know inside, the succession of island-hopping flights seemed endless. Finally, after many long hours aloft, the C-54 touched down at Hickam Field, Hawaii.

To Barr's surprise, instead of being taken to a hospital, he accompanied three of his escorts to the visiting officers' quarters. The two medical officers, aware of Barr's paranoid condition, decided that he should be treated as normally as possible. They invited him to accompany them to the Royal Hawaiian Hotel for lunch and then the Outrigger Club that evening. In his ill-fitting uniform which he had been issued in Kunming, the quiet, skinny repatriate felt out of place and uncertain of himself.

This brief encounter with a carefree world he hadn't seen for over three years helped a little to verify that the war was really over and that he was really in Hawaii, but it was not enough. There were many people of Oriental origin in the streets of Honolulu everywhere he looked. The war had started in Hawaii and the Japanese had boasted before the Tokyo Raid that they would take the islands someday. Maybe they had. After all, he might still be in the South Pacific somewhere and the long flights over water could have been over the China Sea and back to Japanese-held territory as part of their diabolical scheme to further confuse and disorient him.

Next day, Barr and his escorts took a guided tour of the island of Oahu and lunched again at the Royal Hawaiian. While the others joked, relaxed and discussed their war experiences, Barr was uncommunicative. He wanted so desperately to believe that everything was real but to him the evidence was too much against it. Unknown to his escorts, he was fighting a losing battle inside himself. To all outward appearances, in keeping with his silent vow to himself not to cause trouble and be confined again, he appeared normal. Inside, he was absorbing and cataloging the events of each hour and stacking his observations against his preconceived notion that the enemy was controlling every movement, every facial expression and every word that was uttered. Drs. Rich and Millett as well as Col. Decker continually reassured him at every opportunity. By the time they boarded the plane for the final leap to the States, George began to smile and contribute to the conversation, but he was not convinced.

The flight to San Francisco on October 12th was uneventful and after arrival at Hamilton Field, the escorts said goodbye to Barr and left for the nearby separation center in accordance with their orders. Barr was put aboard a bus and rode to the base hospital alone. He had no baggage, no identification, no money and no records. His only possessions were the clothes on his back. The sergeant at the admittance desk asked him questions which he answered hesitantly. Name? Age? Last station and unit of assignment? What was he being treated for? Where was his baggage? Why didn't he have any records?

Obviously disgusted at Barr's feeble attempts to explain his plight, the sergeant shrugged, called a ward orderly and said, "Show the lieutenant to a room and get him some pajamas."

Barr followed mechanically. He was led down several long hallways, up a stairway and eventually into a typical service hospital room containing two high beds, a chair and night stand. There was no one else around.

"Take your clothes off," the orderly commanded. "Put these pajamas on."

Barr slowly unbuttoned his shirt and looked around cautiously as the orderly disappeared. On the night stand was some change and a pocket knife belonging to someone else. That old feeling of being in a cell returned and began to smother him. Again, he was alone in a strange place—a new prison almost exactly like the others he had been in during the last seven weeks. Why hadn't a doctor seen him when he checked in? Why were the belongings of someone else lying there on the nightstand? What was the significance of the knife lying there with American money? Why wasn't anybody else around? Where had the orderly gone?

After several hours, the overwhelming loneliness, the utter hopelessness and the mystery of it all became too much for this emaciated man to take. He had now reached the breaking point. The time and the opportunity had come to end it all. But how?

The pocket knife! That was it! The Japanese, in their twisted Oriental fashion, were going to let him commit hari-kari!

Without thinking any further, Barr seized the knife, pulled it open and jammed the gleaming blade into his chest. Strangely, he felt no pain. Looking down, he expected to see blood gushing out but nothing happened. He pulled the knife out and stared unbelievingly at the small slit it had made. Somehow, the dirty, filthy, evil Japanese had made it impossible to kill himself. He couldn't even bleed. Had the so-called blood plasma he had been given in Peking been used to replace his blood?

Frantic that he should be cheated in his attempt at self-destruction, Barr was now determined to win this last battle with his captors. He opened the window and crawled onto the sill. Looking down, he saw that he was only on the second floor and reasoned that the best he could do from that height was break his legs if he jumped. What other ways could a man kill himself? There were no guns around. Poisons would be locked up. Hanging? Yes. That was it. There was a light fixture in the ceiling. A chair. A rope. What could be used for a rope? A sheet? Too bulky. A belt? Not long enough. Electrical cord? That was it! But where was one?

Barr looked up and down the hall. In the room opposite his he spied a heating lamp. No one was there. The heavy cord on the lamp would be ideal. With the strength of a madman, he ripped the heavy wire from the base of the lamp and made a noose on one end, positioned the chair under the light fixture and stepped on the seat. Carefully tying the other end around the fixture, he placed his head in the loop, tightened it, and kicked the chair away.

Barr's head snapped and the next few seconds were like another nightmare. Huge sparks flew out of the ceiling. There was a crash of glass and metal. Barr crumpled to the floor with a thud that reverberated down the long, quiet corridors to the office of the medical officer of the day.

Five days later, Captain S. H. Green noted the following in report of the incident:

"This 29-year old RAMP,* AAF, unassigned, who was supposed to be one of the original Doolittle fliers, arrived at this hospital via air 12 Oct 45. He had no records nor was he seen by a responsible medical officer. He was routinely placed in the Officer's Section, where he apparently stayed in or near his room most of the day. That night a loud noise was heard, and it was found that he had tried to hang himself from the chandelier which broke. He was immediately transferred to this, the locked mental ward. He was not hurt. Apparently, a mix-up occurred in the evacuation via ATS,** because this man should have been (classified as) Disturbed Mental and the administrative failure almost meant this individual's life.

---

*Repatriated American Military Personnel
**Air Transport Service

"We have kept this man under constant watch ever since he arrived. He is a confused, blocked individual who seldom says more than 2 or 3 words at a time. His affectivity is practically nil and at irregular intervals he becomes very agitated. For example, last night he started screaming that he wanted to die and that he was to be killed and it was necessary to give him sedation to quiet him down. At other times, he stands about restlessly, staring into space."

Barr's view of his attempted suicide and subsequent treatment is understandably different. When he recovered his senses after the light fixture failed to support his weight, he found himself surrounded by medical attendants who forcefully stripped him and put the pajamas on him. He was picked up bodily and taken to Ward S-1 of Letterman General Hospital where he was placed in a padded cell completely devoid of furnishings. The door was slammed shut and his recollections of the next few days were the horribly similar ones of faces at the tiny window and food being shoved through a small trap door. There were no windows to look out of this time, no one to talk to and nothing to do except pace the 6×9-foot cell restlessly. It was the same pattern all over again. The only differences between his present cell and those he had endured in China were the nice, clean padding and the fact that he was well fed.

But the thread of sanity is tenuous. Since his diet was life-sustaining and healthful, he regained his strength. He decided that non-violence always seemed to work with his "captors." Every time he was docile and talked rationally with them, he was eventually allowed some measure of freedom. It worked once more because after five days in the padded cell, he was let out into the locked ward with other patients. The association with other human beings was good therapy for his spirits soared as he listened to the tales of others and was able to compare their stories against his own experiences.

But the brief respite was too soon over. On October 19, the unbelievable chain of unfortunate coincidences for the last of the Doolittle Raiders to return to the States continued. Without preliminary announcement, ward orderlies brought in a half dozen strait jackets and helped the patients put them on. To Barr's amazement, no one objected. He decided that he wouldn't either. Each man, accompanied by one attendant, was then led to a bus. A short time later the bus stopped alongside a train and the men were led aboard a special Pullman car. Jackets were kept on as the train started to move.

Dr. S. H. Green's report showed the medical rationalization behind Barr's transfer:

"His home is in Wisconsin, and we requested that he be sent to Schick General Hospital.* He will be started in restraint because of his unpredictable suicidal outbursts. He will require maximum care en route, and unless this is observed he can be counted upon to injure himself."

As the train picked up speed, Barr and the other patients were put to bed in the Pullman bunks. They were still in their hospital pajamas with the strait jackets still encasing their arms and upper torsos. Restraining sheets covered each man. All they could move was their heads. Since all the blinds were drawn, there was nothing to look at outside the train. It was a prison again—a moving prison this time but a prison nevertheless.

Since struggling was out of the question, Barr lay quietly contemplating his fate. The train clattered and clanked over the rails monotonously through the night. Every hour or so, an attendant came by to check on Barr's condition. Barr complained docilely that he was getting stiff and sore from the restraining sheet but the medic only smiled. Next morning, when Barr repeated the complaint, the medics conferred briefly and took off the sheet to let him walk up and down the length of the darkened car, but with the strait jacket firmly encasing his torso.

"Could I look outside?" Barr asked, casually.

"Sure," the attendant replied. "But you won't see anything."

To prove his point, the white-coated medic raised the curtain. Barr stooped to look out but all he could see was desolate, mountainous countryside. In the distance were taller mountains with snow covering their tops. There was nothing else to see—no houses, no people. Nothing.

The confused Barr was now more than ever convinced that he was the victim of a fantastic scheme to drive him out of his mind. The barren countryside looked exactly like China!

It took three days for the creaking, rattling train to arrive at a siding outside Clinton, Iowa. To a man with a waning reasoning, the sounds that assailed the single ear that he could hear with were cacaphonic and discordant. They only served to further prove the inevitability of his complete breakdown. When the train ground to a final halt on the outskirts of the plains town of Clinton, Barr's ability to reason was about gone.

The bad luck that had dogged George Barr and had brought him to a hospital in a part of the country he had never seen before, had actually been with him all

---

*Barr's "home of record" was actually Yonkers, New York, but since he had enlisted as a Flying Cadet while a student at Northland College, Ashland, Wisconsin, it was assumed that his home was somewhere in the area. Schick General Hospital, in Clinton, Iowa, was the nearest Army hospital.

his life. He had been orphaned at the age of six months when his father disappeared while fishing in Long Island Sound. His mother tried, but was finally unable to support him and his sister Grace, so they were sent to foster homes when George was nine years old. Grace became the special interest of Mrs. Charles H. Towns, a social worker and wife of an accounting executive for Pan-American Airways. George was sent to the Leake and Watts Home School in Yonkers, New York, where he stayed until he was eighteen. He earned extra money serving the Yonkers *Herald-Statesman* on the "city line route."

Mrs. Towns and her husband, themselves childless, "adopted" the Barr children in fact, but not legally. They were determined that they would do what they could to see that these two luckless children were not set adrift without a proper sense of values. George was invited by the Towns' to their house to be with his sister as much as possible. Thus, in the formative years of their lives, George and Grace Barr had guidance and counseling when they needed it most. When Grace, four years older, graduated from high school, the Towns' made it possible for her to go to Northland College, Ashland, Wisconsin. George, an excellent basketball player, also attended Northland where "Red" Barr became very well known by the student body and faculty alike. A. E. Makholm, a college-mate, recalled George in those happy pre-war days:

"George was one of the best-loved men on the campus. Above all, he was relaxed, easy-going, and seemingly bemused about all things. He smiled his big, broad smile constantly and joked and bantered in an inimitable, lighthearted way. Yet his humor was never ribald; it was inevitably quiet, restrained and appropriate. Likewise, his mode of living—while he was always looked upon as 'one of the boys,' his conduct was usually, if not invariably, temperate. I see him now in retrospect as having a sort of 'build-in' gyroscope that held him constantly in an uninhibited yet appropriate and respectful pattern of living. He was, withal, a good student, not an "A" student perhaps, but intelligent and responsive in the classroom.

"When George first appeared on that small, remote Wisconsin campus, most of us were struck by his pronounced Eastern accent and by his slow, almost lazy manner. He seemed incapable of rapid speech or movement. Imagine our surprise on seeing him for the first time on a basketball court. Then this fragile, long-legged, slender if not skinny youth, became a paragon of speed and grace. He was marvelously coordinated. One of the basketball teams on which he played was undefeated for an entire season except for one game, and they averaged over 50 points per game. George played full time as did the other four regulars. The school was too small to provide many players, but these five, by rare coincidence, were outstanding."

After two years at Northland, Barr had laid out for a year to work and earn money to return. He continued his studies majoring in history and math until February, 1941. He was then a semester short of his degree but the lure of the Flying Cadet recruiting posters was strong and he enlisted for pilot training. He was eliminated from pilot training at Muskogee, Oklahoma, but immediately applied for navigator training. He completed courses at Maxwell Field, Alabama, the Pan-American school at Miami, and then transferred to the 34th Bomb Squadron, 17th Bomb Wing, stationed at Pendleton, Oregon. On December 6th, 1941, George Barr realized a dream and was commissioned a second lieutenant in the Army Air Forces. Two days later he began flying sub-hunting missions off the Oregon-Washington coast.

All through his college years and the beginning of his service, Mr. and Mrs. Towns corresponded with him regularly. When his mother died in 1941, the Towns' helped to settle her pitiful estate and advised him on his personal finances. It was their interest, encouragement and advice that stabilized his life and gave it a near-normalcy. They were "family" to him and gave him moral strength when he needed it.

Mrs. Towns, a vibrant, warm person, possessed of prodigious energy, was elated by the news of the Doolittle raid but shocked when she learned that George was one of the crew that was reported missing. George had listed her as "next-of-kin" and it was assumed that she and her husband were foster parents. Reporters hounded her for several days after the news of the Tokyo raid first broke and later when it was announced that George was missing and presumed captured.

When the War Department finally confirmed that the crews of two of Doolittle's B-25's were presumed captured, Mrs. Towns became the go-between for the ten families involved. During the many months following, she clipped every news account that mentioned the Tokyo Raid and wrote long letters of encouragement to the parents of the missing men. She sought information from the International Red Cross, the F.B.I., Army Intelligence, and the repatriated Americans from Japan who arrived on the *Gripsholm* in June, 1942. Every scrap of news was relayed to the parents to keep their hopes up. And when the Japanese announced that some of those captured had been executed, Mrs. Towns never lost hope for George and conveyed her optimism to her correspondents. In addition, hoping that the prisoners were being treated according to the rules of the Geneva Convention and would receive mail, she wrote many cheerful letters addressed to George through the International Red Cross. None were ever delivered, but she had no way of knowing.

When the news was released from China that four of the Doolittle raiders had been found alive, Mr. and Mrs. Towns were overjoyed. "Their" George was safe and would soon be home. They met DeShazer, Nielsen and Hite upon their arrival in the States and sought news of George but the trio had heard nothing about him since the moment they had bid him goodbye in Peking. The Towns' felt better, however, when a cryptic note from George arrived saying he would soon be home but this was followed by weeks of silence. It seemed to them that they were the only people in the world besides an uncle and his sister (by now married and living in Milwaukee) who cared about him or his welfare.

There was at least one other person who cared mightily. That was the man who had led the epic mission that had changed the course of the war in the Pacific. He was now wearing the three-stars of a lieutenant general and had achieved the distinction of being the only reserve officer ever to have risen to three-star rank. The famed Jimmy Doolittle would move heaven and earth to find one of his boys. When Mrs. Towns wrote to him saying that she could not locate George, he dropped everything and started an official search. He assured Mrs. Towns that "we who love George Barr will do everything we can for him. Our objective, however, is not to reform the Army but to find him and help him recover."

But George Barr was incommunicado. He had just arrived at Clinton, Iowa, and was immediately placed in a locked ward with seven other disturbed patients. No doctor visited him and his confused state continued. While Doolittle searched through official channels, Mrs. Towns discovered Barr's whereabouts and notified his sister, now pregnant with her first child. It was decided that her husband, Bill Maas, should make the trip to Clinton instead, accompanied by his father, a physician, who could make an independent observation of George.

The two visitors arrived in Clinton none too soon. George Barr was walking a mental tightrope that threatened to break completely at any moment. When he was ushered into the visitor's lounge, the visitor's faces seemed vaguely familiar to George but much older than he remembered. Bill Maas' face was now scarred, the result of a motorcycle accident. As far as Barr was concerned it could be a trick. Could it be that the Japanese had performed plastic surgery on him to make this man look like his brother-inlaw but had not done a good job of it? He did not believe that his sister would not travel the distance from Milwaukee to Clinton. Was Grace's pregnancy an actuality or just another episode in this Japanese-directed farce?

Doubtful as he was, it was good to see even vaguely familiar faces. Later, he was also visited by several college girl friends and then by Mrs. Towns who had traveled to Iowa as soon as she discovered his whereabouts. But Mrs. Towns didn't look the same to George. He thought she had aged too much and he was conservatively suspicious of her. Yet the visit helped and the words of concern from the one person who had worried so much about his welfare seemed genuine.

Eventually, George was transferred to an open ward. All this time, however, he never saw a doctor, had no money and no clothes. He was a nonentity who seemed to have no future. He was permitted to be alone with his visitors in the ward but was under constant surveillance by medical attendants. He was fading rapidly into a new kind of nothingness. There were the physical comforts of food, light and heat and he had recovered much physical strength. There were a half dozen men in the open ward to talk to now, but he was still confined to the building. It was only a matter of time, he thought, before the Japs would bring down the curtain on the final act. He wondered how long it would be.

One day in late November, there was a commotion outside the ward. Ward boys rushed in and hurriedly straightened up the room.

"Lieutenant Barr, you've got a visitor. Better get cleaned up."

"Who is it?" Barr asked.

"General Doolittle. Says he knows you."

Barr's heart leaped and a surge of joy swept through him he had not known before. He trembled as he stood up and slid his feet into cloth slippers. The door burst open and the man with one of the most famous grins in the world strode in briskly and made his way directly to George, hand outstretched.

"Hi, George! It's good to see you. How are you?" Doolittle said.

The words to answer would not come. Tears welled up instead. Doolittle knew immediately that the last of his lads to come home needed urgent help and he appeared not to notice the moistened eyes. He kept on talking and invited George to go for a walk with him out to an adjoining veranda.

As the two men walked together in the sunlight, George began to find the words that had been stored up inside him so long. He answered Doolittle's questions hesitantly at first, then more easily. The answers came as a shock to the man who had led the most famous air mission of the war. He found it difficult to believe that Barr had not seen a doctor, had no clothes, no money and, in short, seemed to have lost all status as a human being.

Doolittle did not show his concern to Barr, nor convey the fury mounting within him. But he was a man who could not tolerate injustice or inefficient administration and he was the right man to be on hand on this occasion. He accompanied George back to the ward and then went straight to the hospital commander's office and closed the door.

There is no official record of the conversation that ensued but anyone who knew Jimmy Doolittle could easily guess what happened. What is known is that from that moment of that day there was a turning point in the case of disturbed mental patient George Barr. He was suddenly outfitted in a new uniform, complete with the ribbons and overseas stripes he had unknowingly earned, yet never seen. He was promoted to first lieutenant and received a check for over $7,000 in back pay. Best of all, he received the full attention of a psychiatrist who started him on the road to recovery.

Doolittle returned to see George the next day. "George, do you remember the promise I made the day before we left the *Hornet* that when we all got to Chung-king, I'd throw the biggest party you ever saw?"

"Yes, Sir, I do."

"Well, we never had that party, George, because you and all the other fellows couldn't make it. But I'm going to keep my promise now that the war's over. The whole gang is invited to be my guest in Miami on my birthday next month. I want you to come. I'll send an airplane for you. Think you can make it?"

The tall, now smiling redhead, needed no urging. This was the kind of medicine he needed. After Doolittle had extracted a promise from him to come to Miami, the fast-moving airman departed, leaving behind a beaming and happy man who had literally acquired a new lease on life. In the next few weeks he progressed enough to travel accompanied by a qualified medical attendant.

During the second week in December an airplane arrived to transport Barr to Miami. Accompanied by Tech. Sgt. Edward F. Schallenkamp who followed him everywhere, the last of the Tokyo Raiders was reunited with the flying comrades he thought he would never see again. But the adjustment was not to be so easy and while he was happy to be among friends, he still had reservations. He felt out of place among the other Raiders while they relaxed and had a good time. Doolittle, the only one there fully aware of Barr's condition, did everything he could to make him feel at ease. In one of their conversations, Barr mentioned that he would like to visit his alma mater, Northland College, to see old places and faces. The "Boss" made a mental note and when George returned to Iowa, he found that Mrs. Towns and the general had already made arrangements to get him to Ashland, Wisconsin. Old and pleasant memories were awakened as faculty members, students, and townspeople flocked to greet their returned hero and wish him luck. The effect on Barr's outlook was greater than anyone knew. When he returned to Clinton, his confidence was heightened and the suspicions had receded.

The next two years in the life of George Barr were marked by many periods of regression into the old fears and suspicions. At Doolittle's request and Mrs. Towns' suggestion, he was transferred to a former resort lodge at Pauling, New York, which had been turned into a rehabilitation center and then assigned to duty at Mitchel Field, Long Island, New York. With the help of Bob Hite, who had also been assigned to Mitchel Field by Doolittle's order, and Mr. and Mrs. Towns, George gradually regained a balanced outlook. In October, 1946, he met Marcine Andersen and the meeting proved to be a milestone in the recovery of George Barr. Her vibrant, warm personality and depth of understanding provided the magic ingredient that had been missing in his life. They were married in Ashland, Wisconsin, on December 14, 1946.

George Barr autographs photos of the Doolittle Raiders at a reunion in Dayton, Ohio in 1965. Because of extreme malnutrition, Barr was the last of the Raiders to return to the States. He died in 1967.
USAF Photo

Unfortunately, the run of bad luck for George Barr did not end with his marriage. Although he wanted to remain in uniform in the peacetime Air Force, he was retired for physical disability in September, 1947 with the rank of captain. He returned to Northland College and completed the work for his bachelor's degree. He then attended Columbia University and earned his master's degree in physical education after teaching school for a year at Bayfield High School, Bayfield, Wisconsin. Later he became a management analyst for the U.S. Army at Rock Island, Illinois.

The results of the tortures, the imprisonment and the improper diet caused by the Japanese were always with this brave and admirable man. He bore the scars of a leg injury and the infamous finger tortures and awoke at night many times in the throes of a nightmare where he relived the horrible hour he spent in the Japanese strait jacket. But the last of Doolittle's Tokyo Raiders to return from that famous mission was not bitter about his experience, and harbored no resentment toward his former captors. He said he felt lucky to be alive.

The official records in the case of Captain George Barr do not reveal the incredible administrative mixups that occurred to cause him so much misery. Typical of the injustices which dogged him was the award of the Purple Heart. While Hite, DeShazer and Nielsen had been awarded the Purple Heart for wounds received at the hands of the Japanese, Barr never received his. The author called this fact to the attention of another Tokyo Raider, Brigadier General Richard Knobloch, who happened to be deputy commander of the U.S. Air Force Personnel Center at the time. He made a personal crusade out of the matter and the award was finally approved in spite of a "statute of limitations" which prohibits awards later for World War II service. At the 1965 annual Tokyo Raiders reunion in Dayton, Ohio, Jimmy Doolittle presented a surprised George Barr with the medal he had earned over twenty years before.

Barr attended the twenty-fifth reunion of the Tokyo Raiders held at Alameda, California, in April 1967. It marked the first time in many years that all four of the former prisoners were together. George was in good spirits and enjoyed being with those who had shared his misery for so long. Three months later, while attending a school for management analysts, he suffered a severe heart attack and died on July 12, 1967.

EPILOGUE

When Barr, DeShazer, Hite and Nielsen were captured and imprisoned, all were in their twenties. Barr died in July 1967 at age 50. The remaining three are now approaching their eighties. The forty months they spent in primitive cells under barbaric conditions left permanent scars on their memories which time has not completely healed. Their bodies bear the marks of the finger tortures and shin kickings and they still suffer from the after-effects of prolonged malnutrition.

Of the four, only Chase Nielsen elected to remain in the service for a full career. He retired from the Air Force in 1961 as a lieutenant colonel after more than 22 years of active duty and resided in Brigham City, Utah. He was employed at Hill Air Force Base near Salt Lake City as a management engineer and retired from that position in 1981. His first wife, Cleo McCrary, died in February 1995 and he is presently married to the former Phyllis Henderson, also of Brigham City where they reside and enjoy the fine hunting and fishing so abundant in their native state.

Bob Hite remained in the Air Force for two years after World War II was over. He married the former Portia F. Wallace of Enid, Oklahoma and returned to active duty in 1951 to serve during the Korean War. He was stationed at Vance AFB, Oklahoma, as a training squadron commander and later as an air operations officer at a major maintenance depot in Casablanca, Morocco, until 1955. He retired from the Air Force Reserve as a lieutenant colonel and subsequently managed hotels in Camden, Arkansas; Orange and Arlington, Texas; and Muskogee, Oklahoma. He returned to Enid, Oklahoma, and supervised a family hotel and real estate business for several years. He is now retired in Camden, Arkansas.

Jake DeShazer kept his vow to return to Japan as a missionary. He married the former Florence Matheny a year after he was released from prison and completed the requirements for a bachelor's degree at Seattle Pacific College in 1948. They imme-

3-22-08

Jacob DeShazer, Doolittle Raider held as POW, 95

SALEM, Ore. — The Rev. Jacob Daniel "Jake" DeShazer, one of the members of the historic Doolittle Raid on Japan during World War II, has died.

He was 95.

He died Saturday at his Salem home. Ruth Kutrakun, the youngest of DeShazer's children, confirmed the death.

After spending 40 months as a prisoner of war following the raid, Rev. DeShazer returned to Japan intent on forgiving his former captors and converting them to Christianity. Over 30 years, he helped start 23 churches in Japan.

Born Nov. 15, 1912, in Madras to a wheat-farming family, Rev. DeShazer graduated from Madras High School in 1931.

He joined the Army Air Corps at 27, two years before Japan bombed Pearl Harbor. A month after the attack, he volunteered for a secret mission. He was the bombardier aboard the "Bat Out of Hell," one of 16 bombers that launched a surprise attack on Tokyo and other Japanese targets on April 18, 1942.

— ASSOCIATED PRESS

b DeShazer heard a voice which told him the war was going to be over he same voice told him that he should return to Japan and preach the se. Sustained by this, he completed seminary training and returned to ed, as a missionary and served there for thirty years. He is shown at ocation near Nagoya. His wife, Florence, and son stand on his right.

egin evangelistic work and worked there for thirty years. he completed the requirements for a Master of Divinity al Seminary in 1958. He returned to the States for speaking six-year periods in Japan. When he returned permanently to his native Salem, Oregon, in 1978 he was named an assistant pastor at the Salem Free Methodist Church. During his career in Japan, he and Florence got 23 churches established; Florence started three of them from their homes in Nishinomiya, Nagoya, and Tokorozawa.

One of the highlights of DeShazer's career as a missionary was the conversion of Mitsuo Fuchida to Christianity in April 1950. As Fuchida was passing through Shibuya Station in Tokyo, someone stepped out of the crowd and handed him a simple tract—the testimony of DeShazer. Despite his Buddhist heritage, Fuchida bought a Bible and spent several weeks reading it. He pinpointed the date of his acceptance

Mitsuo Fuchida, the Japanese pilot who led the attack on Pearl Harbor in 1941, was converted to Christianity by Jacob DeShazer in 1950. They are shown at their first meeting in Tokyo which was widely publicized. They subsequently traveled and preached together in the U.S.
Photo courtesy Jacob DeShazer

of the Christian message as April 14, 1950, which received worldwide press coverage because it was Fuchida who had led the several hundred planes that had bombed Pearl Harbor on December 7, 1941. It wasn't an easy choice. "Old war buddies came to visit me," Fuchida said, "trying to persuade me to discard 'this crazy idea.' Others accused me of being an opportunist, embracing Christianity only for how it might impress our American victors." Fuchida became a full-time evangelist traveling throughout Japan and the Orient.

To DeShazer, Fuchida's conversion was further proof of the miracles promised in the Bible he had read so voraciously in prison. He invited Fuchida to the United States and the two of them toured the country with their joint message of hope and faith. Fuchida died in 1976.

DeShazer told the author, "Reading the Bible in the Japanese prison was the best thing that ever happened to me." Although retired now and one of the oldest surviving members of the original eighty of Doolittle's Tokyo Raiders, he continues to

Chase J. Nielsen and George Barr, share a joke with General James H. "Jimmy" Doolittle at the dedication of a Tokyo Raider display at Wright-Patterson Air Force Base in 1963. USAF PHOTO

accept speaking engagements from churches and veterans organizations throughout the country.

While Jake DeShazer was the only one of the four survivors to enter the ministry, the other three freely admit that the message of the Bible they were given after Meder's

General Jimmy Doolittle and the author autograph copies of *Four Came Home* during a Tokyo Raider Reunion at Oakland, California. Glines is also the author of *Doolittle's Tokyo Raiders* and *The Doolittle Raid*. Photo: Holt Graphic Arts

death deeply affected their personal religious philosophies. They feel their survival was due to the messages of hope and forgiveness they found in its tattered pages. They harbor no permanent resentment against their captors and are grateful to God for their survival and eventual release.

In the years following their release, all four men reflected on their captivity during personal appearances many times. They are usually asked what lessons they learned. As a result, they jointly composed the following article based on their experiences and observations exclusively for this book. They received the Freedoms Foundation Award in 1967 for this article and "For outstanding achievement in bringing about a better understanding of the American way of life."

If American servicemen will heed their advice should they ever be captured by a hostile force, chances are great that they will return to home and loved ones with full knowledge that they had upheld the honor and traditions of the American fighting man.

PRISON REFLECTIONS
by
George Barr
Jacob D. DeShazer
Robert L. Hite
Chase J. Nielsen

The four of us were never mentally prepared for imprisonment by the Japanese when we volunteered for the Tokyo Raid. We received no formal instruction in the provisions of the Geneva Convention of 1929 regarding treatment of war prisoners. We did not know what to expect in the way of prison conditions. And we did not realize how much the human body and mind could take and still survive.

Many years have passed since we blasted off the decks of the *Hornet*, dropped our bombs on Japan and were captured by the Japanese in China. During our three years and four months of captivity, we learned some basic lessons about democracy, religion and ourselves, which may seem strange since we spent most of that time in solitary confinement.

We learned the ultimate meaning of democracy and the freedoms that a democratic government represents. In the hundreds of lonely hours we spent trying to retain our sanity by reviewing the things we learned in grammar and high school, often reluctantly, one of the documents we remembered and recited to ourselves was the Declaration of Independence:

> We hold these truths to be self-evident, that all men are created equal, that they are endowed by their Creator with certain unalienable Rights, that among these are Life, Liberty and the pursuit of Happiness. That to secure these rights. Governments are instituted among Men, deriving their just powers from the consent of the governed . . .

The meaning of those words really comes home to you when you are confined by a brutal enemy who totally rejects the concept of individual liberty. Those principles heartened the soldiers of the Revolutionary War and they serve as a time-tested standard for the American fighting man today. They served to help us through some of our most doubtful moments.

We were not what you would call religious men before we were captured. We went to Sunday School and church when we were kids like thousands of others. We memorized Bible verses and listened to sermons and said grace at meals. We knew the Ten Commandments. But we never really understood the meaning behind those

General Jimmy Doolittle was happiest when he was with his fellow Tokyo Raiders at their annual reunions. Here he chats with Robert Hite (center) as Chase Nielsen looks on. USAF PHOTO

words and the source of strength they represented in our lives until we were reduced to a minimum survival level and had to live with our own thoughts and memories for so long.

The four of us began to recognize the true meaning of religion when we were given the Bible to read. We found in its ripped and faded pages a source of courage and faith we never realized existed. The verses we memorized as children suddenly came alive and became as vital to us as food. We put our trust in the God we had not really accepted before and discovered that faith in His word could carry us through the greatest peril of our lives.

Our United States, when still a young nation, proudly proclaimed its position to the world in its slogan "In God We Trust." It is the only nation on earth that has its entire heritage resting on the firm foundation of faith in a God who rules the world with justice and mercy. American military men and women must believe that with all their heart and soul. If they do, they will find that God will not forsake those who trust Him and live by His Commandments.

Centuries ago a soldier wrote the 23rd Psalm. Believe us, we said that verse thousands of times to ourselves and it gave us great comfort. Ever since it was first written, its message has echoed in the minds and hearts of other military men in succeeding generations:

> Yea, though I walk through the valley of the shadow of death, I will fear no evil; for thou art with me; thy rod and thy staff, they will comfort me.

Another lesson we learned but not until we were released is that an American fighting man must place a trust in his government. He must remember that no American prisoner of war will be forgotten by the United States. He is assured that every available means will be employed by our government to establish contact with, to support and obtain the release of all prisoners of war. And he should remember that the laws of the United States provide for the support and care of the dependents of members of the Armed Forces including those who become prisoners of war.

It is natural for a prisoner to worry about whether his government really cares about him and his family. But his mind can be relieved on that score. We found that literally thousands of people, including the President of the United States, had worked long and hard to communicate with us and determine our fate. Our families were kept informed as best they could be in time of war. We worried but we needn't have because the American people have voted laws into being which assure that the individual and his family will be protected.

We followed with great personal interest the plight of the thousands of Americans who were taken prisoner during the Korean and Vietnam wars. While the Japanese Kempei Tai torture professionals had been rough on us, it was evident that the communists in Korea had introduced new and more scientific tortures into the treatment of POWs. Besides the physical tortures, the communists introduced "brainwashing" and induced some prisoners to become informers and collaborators by exploiting their natural fears and worries.

Despite the wide publicity given to informers and collaborators, they did not set the pattern for our fighting men in Korea. The large majority of American prisoners resisted the enemy in the highest tradition of the service and our country.

One of the lessons learned from the Korean War was that American fighting men must be mentally prepared to resist the brainwashing techniques should they ever be captured. We were not prepared for capture during World War II and neither were the thousands of Americans during the Korean War. As a result of the bitter lessons of these two conflicts, President Dwight D. Eisenhower signed into law a Code of Conduct for members of the Armed Forces of the United States on August 17, 1955. (As a result of the war in Vietnam, the Code was changed slightly in 1977 in only one instance and was made gender neutral in 1988.)

Today, every American soldier, sailor, airman and marine is required to learn this Code of Conduct and receive "specific training and instruction designed to better equip him to counter and withstand all enemy efforts against him, and shall be fully instructed as to the behavior and obligations expected of him during combat or captivity." The Code itself is a set of standards which we wish we had received as a guide for us in captivity. If we had been given such a code, perhaps we would have acted differently. At least it would have put into words what we came to conclude the hard way:

I. I am an American in the forces which guard my country and our way of life. I am prepared to give my life in their defense.

II. I will never surrender of my own free will. If in command, I will never surrender the members of my command while they still have the means to resist.

III. If I am captured I will continue to resist by all means available. I will make every effort to escape and aid others to escape. I will accept neither parole nor special favors from the enemy.

IV. If I become a prisoner of war I will keep faith with my fellow prisoners. I will give no information nor take part in any action which might be harmful to my comrades. If I am senior, I will take command. If not, I will obey the lawful orders of those appointed over me and will back them up in every way.

V. When questioned, should I become a prisoner of war, I am required to give name, rank, service number and date of birth. I will evade answering further questions to the utmost of my ability. I will make no oral or written statements disloyal to my country and its allies or harmful to their cause.

VI. I will never forget that I am an American fighting for freedom, responsible for my actions, and dedicated to the principles which make my country free. I will trust in my God and in the United States of America.

Each year the surviving members of Doolittle's Tokyo Raiders hold a reunion. The silver goblets shown above are used for toasts to the deceased crew members whose goblets are turned down. The last two surviving members will drink a final toast from the bottle of brandy. Between reunions, the goblets are displayed at the Air Force Academy at Colorado Springs, Colorado. Photo by C. V. Glines

We are unequivocally in favor of the Code and the training connected with it that our armed forces now receive. But the importance of the Code extends far beyond the limits of a single war or a single group of Americans. Every American citizen must share the responsibility for preserving our freedoms and our way of life. In modern warfare, the home front is an extension of the fighting front. Courage and loyalty are expected of every American and we must not take our freedoms for granted. Threats to those freedoms must be met with appropriate American weapons—not only the physical weapons of war but mental and moral weapons as well. It is the latter which are supplied by the moral strength, will and minds of the American people.

The Code of Conduct calls upon all members of the Armed Forces to stand firm, without crumbling and yielding, in the face of enemy pressure and torture. It follows the premise that every American has, in the values that have shaped him, in the substance of his own experience, the strength it takes to live by the Code and meet whatever test the enemy may force upon him.

The specific source of strength may vary from person to person. For some it is in a strong faith in God. For others it may be the love of country or family. For still others, it may be simply an unflinching pride. It may be all of these together. But whatever it is for anyone faced with capture, we feel that a person who lives by the Code will find in it a reservoir of strength that will enable him to endure with honor any crisis thrust upon him.

The four survivors of Japanese imprisonment pose at a Tokyo Raider reunion in Los Angeles with Brig. Gen. John A. Hilger, second in command of the Raiders. (L to R) Chase J. Nielsen, Jacob DeShazer, Hilger, Robert L. Hite, George Barr. USAF Photo

We have concluded that the concept of liberty—American liberty—is a religion. It is a thing of the spirit and exemplifies the highest ideals ever expressed for the betterment of mankind. Our buddies—Faktor, Dieter, Fitzmaurice, Spatz, Hallmark, Farrow and Meder—died to perpetuate those ideals. We do not think they died in vain.

Retired Navy Chief E. Franklin Owens, attends a memorial marker at a Darlington, S.C. cemetery in honor of Lt. William G. Farrow. Owens had become friends with Farrow on board the *Hornet*. He has maintained the marker for over 35 years. PHOTO COURTESY E. FRANKLIN OWENS

The Doolittle Tokyo Raiders display at the Air Force Museum at Wright-Patterson AFB, Dayton, Ohio. Various photographs and memorabilia of the participants are vividly displayed to tell the story of the mission. The parachute overhead was used by Lt. Jack Sims when he bailed out over China. AFM

INDEX

About the Author

Carroll V. Glines is the author of 30 books on aviation and military subjects, including *Jimmy Doolittle: Master of the Calculated Risk* and *Doolittle's Tokyo Raiders*. Currently the curator of the Doolittle Library at the University of Texas at Dallas, Glines was an Air Force pilot and had extensive experience in the Army Air Forces during World War II. He retired from the military in 1968 with the rank of colonel. As a civilian he is the co-holder of national and international speed records in fixed-wing, amphibian and rotary-wing aircraft.

Glines has received writing awards from Freedoms Foundation, Aviation/Space Writers Association, International Association of Business Communicators, International Labor Press Association, Society of National Association Publications, and Alaska Press Association. He received the Max Steinbock Award from International Labor Press Association for "best journalistic effort which exemplifies a human spirit" and Lauren D. Lyman Award from Aviation/Space Writers Association for "integrity, accuracy and excellence in reporting and writing, deep understanding of others, and devotion to the best interests of the aviation industry."